Morocco - Tunisia

2

++++++++++++++ *National Planning Series* ++++++++++++++

BERTRAM M. GROSS, GENERAL EDITOR

++++++++++++++++++++++++++++++++++++++ +++++++++++++++++++++++++

DOUGLAS ELLIOTT ASHFORD is Associate Professor of Public and International Affairs in the Graduate School of Business and Public Administration at Cornell University. He has held teaching positions at Princeton, Indiana, and Johns Hopkins Universities and was Area Studies Director of the Moroccan Peace Corps II group at Utah State University in 1963.

Professor Ashford collected material for the present volume while engaged in research and travel in Morocco and Tunisia under an ACLS-SSRC Fellowship. His other published works include *Political Change in Morocco, Perspectives of a Moroccan Nationalist,* and numerous articles in such professional journals as *Western Political Quarterly, Middle East Journal, American Political Science Review,* and *World Politics.*

‡‡‡

Morocco - Tunisia
Politics and Planning

DOUGLAS ELLIOTT ASHFORD

Preface by

BERTRAM M. GROSS

SYRACUSE UNIVERSITY PRESS

First Edition 1965

Acknowledgment

This and other volumes in the National Planning
Series were initiated with the encouragement and
support of Stephen K. Bailey, Dean of the Maxwell
Graduate School of Citizenship and Public Affairs,
Syracuse University, and of his predecessor, Harlan
Cleveland. They have been made possible through
a grant from the Ford Foundation for cross-cultural
research by the Maxwell School. In the final editing
of the manuscript valuable assistance was provided
by Sherry Siracuse and James Gies.

BERTRAM M. GROSS

Manufactured in the United States of America

Contents

From Symbolism to Action: *A Prefatory Comment* by
BERTRAM M. GROSS   vii
Symbolic and Ritualistic Planning   viii
The Symbolism of "Developmental Socialism"   xi
The Ritualism of Development Economics   xv
The Power Politics of Planning   xviii

I.   Where Planning Begins   1

II.   Political Forces in the Commitment to Planning   7
Morocco: Nationalist Disintegration and Political Indecision   8
Tunisia: Nationalist Solidarity and Political Procrastination   17

III.   Participation and the Planning Effort   30
Morocco: Reluctance and Indecision   31
Tunisia: Anticipation and Reform   38

IV.   An Approach through the Social Sciences   46

Notes to Chapters   51

Selected Bibliography   59

Index   63

From Symbolism to Action

This is the first truly comparative study of national planning among developing noncommunist nations.

Until now the only cross-national empirical survey has been Peter Wiles's brilliant *The Political Economy of Communism*,[1] which concentrates upon the Soviet Union and its neighbors in Eastern Europe. The major contribution of Wiles's more intensive study lies in the use of new forms of economic analysis, while Douglas Ashford limits himself to the political aspects of economic planning in Morocco and Tunisia. But the great value of both authors' work lies in their careful comparison of planning experience in countries that have much in common. This leads to more meaningful conclusions than are possible by examining one country alone or, at the other extreme, making panoramic comparisons on a world-wide basis.

It may well be hoped that the Wiles–Ashford example will be followed by many others. The time has already come, for example, for a comparative study of national planning in India (which seems to be encountering increasing difficulties) and Pakistan (which seems to be making considerable progress). Another fruitful comparison—now made more feasible by the first two Latin American volumes [2] in this National Planning Series—would be between Latin America's two leaders in economic growth: Venezuela, with a sophisticated planning mechanism under CORDIPLAN, and Mexico, with no institutionalized planning machinery that can readily be observed. Let us even look forward to an extension of Ashford's inquiry to include Algeria also, and thus the entire Maghrib.

For those who may equate scholarly work with long and exhaustive (and exhausting) treatises, the very brevity of Ashford's study may tend to conceal the importance of his central themes:

[1] (Cambridge: Harvard University Press, 1962.)

[2] John Friedmann, *Venezuela: From Doctrine to Dialogue* (Syracuse: Syracuse University Press, 1965), and Robert J. Shafer, *Mexico: Mutual Adjustment Planning* (Syracuse: Syracuse University Press, 1965).

symbolic and ritualistic planning, and power politics. These themes have tremendous significance for those involved either in the guidance of national economic change or in research and theory on this increasingly widespread aspect of man's life on this planet. Accordingly, I shall touch briefly upon some of their implications.

Symbolic and Ritualistic Planning

Ashford's discussion of "symbolic change" and "ritual change" (pp. 46–49) is one of the rare occasions when the language of anthropology has been used in an area traditionally dominated by the more narrow and aseptic language of economics. In his 2 x 2 matrix on social and attitudinal change, Ashford points out the ever-present possibility that national planning may be either symbolic or ritualistic. Symbolic planning occurs when proplanning attitudes develop as "a convenient psychological adjustment to avoid changing behavior." Ritualistic planning occurs when behavior is actually changed in specific ways without being backed by attitudinal adjustments. Neither kind of planning is likely to create sustained support at the local level, nor is it likely to provide a lasting commitment to the planning process. Symbolic planning is strengthened by changed behavior, whereas ritualistic planning is strengthened by changed attitudes. In either case, the implication of Ashford's analysis is that institutionalized planning requires participation in the planning process by an ever-widening circle of key individuals and organizations. A central planning agency by itself can never be very effective either in formulating or implementing significant plans for rapid economic development. Its work can be of genuine value only if it is an integral part of a complex central guidance cluster which is itself closely linked with major power centers throughout the social system.[3]

It would be a great (although natural) error for the reader to interpret the Ashford style of analysis as applicable only to the so-called developing nations. Anthropologists, unfortunately, have accustomed too many of us to thinking of rituals, rites, and ceremonies as occurring only in "traditional" or "primitive" societies

[3] The major roles in central guidance clusters are analyzed in Bertram M. Gross, "The Managers of National Economic Change," in *Public Administration and Democracy: Essays in Honor of Paul H. Appleby,* ed. Roscoe, Martin (Syracuse: Syracuse University Press, 1965).

where these phenomena are more visible to the naked eye of the Western observer. We find it much more difficult to see these phenomena in the more industrially developed societies. Yet in the United States of America, Western Europe, and all of Eastern Europe, we find the same problem that Ashford defines: *relating changing values to changing behavior in the context of development and planning* (p. 46). Indeed, in the industrialized societies, many of which are already in full-blown transition to postindustrialism, some aspects of social change are far more rapid than in the preindustrial and industrializing nations.

As yet, the only serious study of symbolism and ritualism in an industrial society is Thurman Arnold's classic—and ever-exciting—*The Folklore of Capitalism.*[4] Concentrating upon the American corporation, Arnold points out that rituals and ceremonies are needed to reconcile the conflicting ideals of members or help accommodate ideals to practical necessities.[5] He points to the frequent failure of intellectuals as administrators because of their over-emphasis upon "rigorous dialectic and the so-called intellectual skills" at times when effective action requires, instead, some skillful development of rites and ceremonies.[6] Following in Arnold's footsteps, I have suggested that all truly modern organizations *invariably* use twentieth-century forms of rites of passage, of intensification, of divination and of sanctification—and even, as with academic promotion and tenure, cults of affliction.[7] In the case of national planning, careful observation might lead to finding such phenomena in the central guidance clusters of all countries. Thus, in looking back upon my own experience with the President's Council of Economic Advisers during its first five years of existence (1946–51), I have no difficulty in finding such illustrations as the following:

1. Rites of passage: The grueling trial period before the Council and its staff were finally accepted as a part of the Executive Office of the President;

2. Rites of intensification: The recurrent speeches and

---

[4] (New Haven: Yale University Press, 1937.)
[5] *Ibid.*, pp. 350–56.
[6] *Ibid.*, pp. 385–93.
[7] Bertram M. Gross, "Rituals" in Chap. 28, "Observance of Codes," *The Managing of Organizations* (New York: Free Press, 1964), pp. 723–25.

meetings and other activities needed (but not always forthcoming) to re-emphasize lagging dedication to the maximum
employment goal of the Employment Act of 1946;

3. Rites of divination: The elaborate intellectual gyrations
through which, in trying to predict the future, we gave differ-
ential emphasis to each element in the tripartite proposition
that the economy might improve, deteriorate, or stay the
same;

4. Rites of sanctification: The Cabinet sessions and inter-
departmental memoranda which legitimated the policy decisions of the President and his close associates; and

5. Cults of affliction: The grillings given the Council by
the House Appropriations Subcommittee and the castigations
given the Chairman of the Council, Leon H. Keyserling, by
academic economists who resented his lack of a Ph.D. in economics.

Returning to Morocco and Tunisia, we can find interesting support for Ashford's observations. Albert Waterston's earlier study of
planning in Morocco clearly suggests the symbolic and ritualistic
nature of many Moroccan planning organs. Thus, since August
1960, the Superior Planning Council "has not been convened by
the Government." [8] Although the plan called for regional study and
planning societies, "no regional study and planning societies have
been established since the inception of the Five Year Plan." [9] An
Interministerial Economic Commission called for in the plan has also
been inoperative.[10] With high symbolic fervor the law creating the
Division of Economic Coordination and Planning "empowered it
to supervise the execution of all plans and programs in accordance
with the directives of the Superior Planning Council." [11] Yet the
legally authorized planning division "has not had the status and
support to carry out the functions assigned to it." [12] Thus, according to Waterston, it "has become little more than a research organization. . . . About four-fifths of its personnel are employed
in gathering and collating basic statistical material which, although
required by planners, is not directly related to the planning func-

[8] *Planning in Morocco* (Baltimore: Johns Hopkins Press, 1962), p. 37.
[9] *Ibid.*, p. 36.
[10] *Ibid.*, p. 37.
[11] *Ibid.*, p. 39.
[12] *Ibid.*, p. 47.

tion." [13] At the same time it "has tended to concentrate too much attention on input-output matrices, mathematical growth models . . . and similarly advanced econometric formulations at the expense of essential, though more mundane, investigations which could yield results of more immediate value." [14]

Ashford's suggestion that Tunisia is moving at last, after early delays, toward genuine institutionalization of planning is supported, in part, by the recent Perroux-Debeauvais report to a United Nations group on planning in that country.[15] Here we find that the present planning machinery in Tunisia is "remarkable especially for the relative buoyancy of its administrative apparatus. This trait is especially noticeable at the level of the higher cadres. A small group of senior officials, most of them young, perform a variety of functions, and the daily execution of their tasks bears the stamp of multiple links (common education, political allegiance, and experience) which unite them. A directing team has thus been constituted whose convergent action, by reason of these special links, gives Tunisian planning its true visage, even more, perhaps, than the observance—in practice the very strict observance—of rules and procedures." [16] The people are brought into plan preparation through the "traditional procedure of consultation with agencies especially established for that purpose." [17] Also, "new methods of mass communication which, at the first stage of development, aim at informing the people about the major options of national and regional economic policy, but which are eventually designed to create conditions for a dialogue between the 'base' and the 'summit'. . . . It is significant that Tunisia is one of the few countries in the world where any citizen can purchase the text of the plan from any newsstand." [18]

THE SYMBOLISM OF "DEVELOPMENTAL SOCIALISM"

If any single phrase were to be used to describe the underlying philosophy of the Tunisian government, it would be "Neo-Des-

[13] *Ibid.,* p. 48.

[14] *Ibid.,* p. 47.

[15] François Perroux and Michel Debeauvais, *The Administration of Planning in Tunisia,* Addendum to the Report of Preliminary Study for U.N. Meeting of Experts on Administrative Aspects of National Development Planning, February 1964 (mimeo).

[16] *Ibid.,* p. 3.

[17] *Ibid.,* p. 12.

[18] *Ibid.,* pp. 13, 18.

tourian socialism." The same phrase could also be applied to Tunisian planning. As Ashford points out, "national planning is generally a consequence of socialistic thought" (p. 1). Moreover, President Bourguiba's espousal of national planning was preceded by a few years of strenuous pressure for such action by the General Union of Tunisian Workers (UGTT). "The UGTT's Secretary General, Ahmed Ben Salah, advocated a distinctly socialist line of economic development and felt that the workers were entitled to special recognition for their sacrifices on behalf of the Neo-Destour" (p. 21). Some years later Ben Salah himself was made head of the "superministry" of planning and finance (pp. 27–28).

In Marxist and neo-Marxist thought and practice, "socialism" refers to a regime based upon public ownership of the means of production. In only slightly watered-down form, this version of socialism was advocated by a 1960 UGTT report calling for " 'an economic system based on cooperation and popular association of investment funds assuring the socialization of the means of production' " (p. 26). In contrast, the actual practice of planning under Neo-Destourian socialism has been rather far removed from "the socialization of the means of production." Bourguiba made it clear from the very beginning that "the plan would not eliminate or obstruct private initiative." Tremendous efforts were made to win support for the plan from merchants and private landowners.

In presenting socialistic ideals as the basis of its economic planning activities, Tunisia is no exception. In Morocco Bouabid and the National Union Party also advocate socialism. Below the Sahara the key phrase for developmental planning is "African socialism." In Tanganyika the key word—not readily translatable from Swahili—is "Ujaama." [19] Indian planning is officially based on "democratic socialism." Yet, in most of these countries, as in Tunisia, the word has little reference to the socialization of the means of production. For President Nyerere of Tanganyika, for example, "socialism is an attitude of mind which inclines men toward a deeply felt sense of obligation for the welfare of their fellow men." [20] For Kenya's Tom Mboya African socialism refers to "the African's

[19] Fred G. Burke, "Tanganyika: The Search for Ujaama," in *African Socialism*, eds. William H. Friedland and Carl G. Rosberg, Jr. (Stanford: Stanford University Press, 1964).
[20] *Ibid.*, p. 194.

thought processes and cosmological ideas which regard man, not as a social means, but as an end and entity in society." [21]

Moreover, in most noncommunist developing countries, as in Tunisia, socialism in practice turns out to be a far cry from socialization. First of all, "present underdeveloped countries, as shaped by the past, are overwhelmingly private enterprise economies. The public share in income, wealth and employment is small. And large areas of economic activity are almost entirely locally independent and relatively untouched by the hand of the central government. . . . In countries with per capita incomes of less than $100, the share of government runs customarily from 6 or 7 to about 15 percent. In Western countries with per capita incomes of, say $800 and above, the figure customarily varies between 20 and 30 percent." [22] In the United States of America, presumably the citadel of private enterprise, government purchases of goods and services in 1964 amounted to more than 22 per cent of the gross national product.[23] Second, although government plays a very large role in new investment, much of this investment is directed toward the initiation or expansion of private enterprises or cooperative enterprises not owned by the state. Although governmental controls are extensive, particularly with respect to foreign currency and import licenses, entrepreneurs have learned to live with them—indeed, often to escape them rather effectively. Although some countries started out with a doctrinaire belief in nationalization, experience has led to an ever-widening realization that changes in the formal structure of ownership do not automatically solve the problems of enterprise management.

But this does not mean that "developmental socialism" is mere empty talk. On the contrary, it is extremely meaningful as an expression of certain fundamental attitudes toward the future of developing societies. Thus, in the socialism of such men as Nehru (India), Nyerere (Tanganyika), Mboya (Kenya), Bourguiba (Tunisia), Bouabid (Morocco), and to some extent even Nkrumah (Ghana) and Touré (Guinea), one may find certain basic elements. For all these men and the movements they have led, the

[21] Ibid., p. 206.

[22] Edward S. Mason, Economic Planning in Underdeveloped Areas (New York: Fordham University Press, 1958), pp. 7, 12.

[23] Council of Economic Advisers, Economic Indicators, August 1965 (Washington: U.S. Government Printing Office, 1965), p. 2.

term "socialism" has been a glowing symbol of (1) social justice
and higher living standards, (2) achieved through more or less
democratic processes, (3) without colonialism, and (4) through
the presumably rational processes of national planning.

Insofar as the two first points are concerned, the goals are not
very different from those of the "welfare state" developed by the
so-called capitalist democracies. Indeed, in view of their relative
poverty, none of the countries advocating "developmental socialism" contemplate getting anywhere near welfare state standards
during the next few generations. Insofar as democratic processes
are concerned, both the goal and the practice cover a much wider
range of variations than can be discussed in this context. Suffice it
to say that both Neo-Destourian socialism and Ujaama contemplate
widespread participation in the making of decisions—albeit within
the framework of a single-party system. On the other hand, since
the welfare state societies have been the colonial powers of the past,
the third of these points has become particularly important. Developmental socialism has thus increasingly come to symbolize independence from colonial rule and the development of native (public or private) enterprise as against foreign enterprise or foreign
control. As a symbol of self-respect and national dignity, the banner of socialism becomes all the more meaningful whenever leaders in these countries are subjected to Western pressures toward
private interests or Western lectures on the virtues of private enterprise. Finally, while developmental socialism implies national
planning, it provides no guidelines whatsoever as to how national
planning can be conducted. In essence, we are left then with a
form of symbolism which—by expressing attitudes favorable to
social justice, independence, democracy, and planning—paves the
way toward significant changes in behavior.[24]

[24] In contrast, one might consider the significance of the "free enterprise" symbolism used persistently through the New Deal, Fair Deal, and New Frontier
periods in the United States and continued in the present "Great Society" era.
Although often attacked by conservatives as "creeping socialism," the social
welfare measures adopted during these "free enterprise" regimes might indeed be
regarded as "walking socialism" (a mathematician might call it a "random walk")
compared with the truly creeping pace of the socialists in most developing
nations.

THE RITUALISM OF DEVELOPMENT ECONOMICS

As the economics of planned development becomes more ma-
ture, socialist symbolism invariably declines. Older socialist doc-
trines on the virtues of nationalization give way to pragmatic prob-
ings of the relative advantages and disadvantages of different kinds
of enterprises: private, cooperative, mixed, or public. Market mechanisms and pricing systems are exploited to serve public interests.
Within the public sector "modern management" becomes the major
slogan. The development plan itself sets forth the goals of higher
living standards and social justice. The banner of socialism may
still be unfurled, but mainly as a symbol of anticolonial nationalism.

At the same time development economics has its own cere-
monial, ritualistic, and symbolic aspects. The "number magic" of
econometric projections, for example, may play a powerful role in
legitimating goals for investment, exports, or import replacement.
This role may have no relation whatsoever (or perhaps an inverse
one) to the statistical reliability of the numbers used, the validity
of the theory on which the projections are based, or the extent to
which they are understood by policy makers.

Ashford's direct handling of the politics of planned development highlights, by contrast, a still more subtle form of intellectual
ritualism in development economics. This is the ritualistic style in
which development economists tend to approach the important subject of plan implementation. Interested as they are (and indeed
must be) in evaluating actual performance under development
plans, they cannot afford to ignore the subject of implementation.
Nor can they possibly ignore the fact that implementation requires,
in addition to economic plans that are technically implementable,
institutional change, managerial capacity, and political action. Yet,
as professional economists, they have rarely concerned themselves with these rich and burgeoning fields. Nor have they seen
fit to call upon the services of, or associate themselves with, out-
standing leaders in the analysis of social institutions, management,
or politics. As the currently accepted experts in the planning of
economic development, they have for the most part preferred to
"go it alone."

In order to go it alone, however, development economists have used various ritualistic devices of paying obeisance to these vital aspects of implementation. Thus, institutional change will be mentioned casually—but without any clear conception of what social institutions are or how they may be built or transformed. For example, a major UN report, *Planning for Economic Development*,[25] begins with a few generalities about the interest of developing nations in "economic and social structures" and "problems of structural adaptation." The economist authors of the report then quickly drop the subject. Problems of management and administration cannot be avoided so easily. Here the ritual usually involves the solemn use of public administration concepts that were outmoded a quarter of a century ago. Considerable space is given to primitive discussion of the "location" of planning agencies, the formal divisions of labor (without genuine role analysis) and the elaboration of mechanisms and procedures. The favorite procedures are those involved in evaluation, appraisal, and reporting systems—invariably with no attention to the profound problems involved in connection with the criteria of evaluation, the collection of information relative to such criteria, the use of such information, the identity of the evaluator, or the delicate relation that always exists between evaluator and evaluatee.[26] All this leads—and the UN report *Planning for Economic Development* is a prime example—to a rare combination of dullness and irrelevance to implementation.[27]

Insofar as political action is concerned, the ritualism of development economics seems to center around the concept of *will*—a great, glittering generality retrieved from abstractions of nineteenth-century psychology, political philosophy, and metaphysics. Thus, in the same UN report, we find that "far more important than the technical competence in the formulation of plans" are

[25] United Nations Department of Economic and Social Affairs, *Planning for Economic and Social Development*, Report of an international group of experts (New York: United Nations, 1965).

[26] A brief summation of the difficulties and pitfalls involved in evaluation processes at the simpler level of formal organizations may be found in "Evaluating: Basis of Control" in Chap. 29 of Bertram M. Gross, *The Managing of Organizations* (New York: Free Press, 1964), pp. 794–804.

[27] *Ibid.*, Chap. 2, "The Implementation of Plans." This entire chapter concentrates mainly upon the formulation of policies with respect to savings, foreign exchange, public investment, social programs, agriculture, and industry. With plan formulation conceived of narrowly as the development of macroeconomic objectives, the formulation of somewhat more specific objectives is then called "implementation."

"the *will* to pursue effective policies" and "the *will* to select effective policies for the realization of national objectives." [28] (Italics added.) In a typical report of the Economic Commission for Latin America, a prescription for plan implementation in Bolivia is given in similar terms: "What is chiefly required is the 'will to plan' on the part of the political authorities." [29]

In none of these discussions is any whispering hint given of the many forms of resistance to economic development or of the sober, sometimes brutal, realities of what is involved in mobilizing and using power to overcome such resistance. Rather, the "will to plan" of the development economists calls forth the image of a strong and noble national leader who consults regularly with his economists, accepts their advice instead of "playing politics" and by the clarity of his high resolve and the vigor of his executive decisiveness gets things done. If things do not go well, from this point of view, it is because of "the absence of a consistent development policy." [30] Or it is because less noble objectives have interfered. Thus, in one economist's review of development planning in Southeast Asia we find that at the heart of the problem is the fact that economic development has not been espoused as the major national goal. Indeed, energies and resources have been diverted from economic development to such matters as nation-building, international prestige, and national security.[31]

The intellectual ritualism of such observations provides a surrogate for the direct confrontation of delicate political issues and an excuse for not becoming familiar with the growing literature on political development, management, and institution-building. At the same time, it enables economists to recognize explicitly the existence and importance of noneconomic factors in economic growth. A temporary, halfway house is thus provided for economists who set out on the long road of analyzing the processes of economic and social change. The next generation of such analysts, it is to be hoped, may yet be able to use the tools of any relevant

[28] *Ibid.,* p. 5.
[29] "The Economic Development of Bolivia," *Economic Bulletin for Latin America,* October 1957, p. 44.
[30] Waterston, *Planning in Morocco,* p. 49.
[31] Clair Wilcox, *The Planning and Execution of Economic Development in Southeast Asia,* Harvard University Center for International Affairs, Occasional Papers in International Affairs, No. 10 (Cambridge: Center for International Affairs, January 1965), pp. 33, 35–37.

disciplines instead of confining themselves to those variables for which a traditional discipline has accustomed them.

THE POWER POLITICS OF PLANNING

Ashford's straightforward report on the political aspects of national economic planning provides an excellent introduction for those who want to get behind such phrases as "will" and "commitment to a consistent development policy."

First of all, Ashford shows the importance of close relations between a central planning agency and the political forces interested in economic development. In Morocco the ineffectiveness of the Superior Planning Council is attributable to the fact that "political forces have been largely excluded from the planning process." In Tunisia the National Planning Council started out as a political device to "explain delay and distract critics." Later, with the dominant party being converted into an organization fighting for economic development, the new secretary of state for planning and finance became a vigorous center for guided development. The implications of nonsupport or support by political forces, moreover, reach far beyond the activities of any single agency. In Morocco, where this support has not been forthcoming, "planning activity has been sporadic and erratic . . . [and] nearly all Moroccan proposals for reform and development projects have been inordinately delayed." In contrast, Tunisia "has managed to reorganize her economic institutions to fill planning needs. The administration has aso been reformed and sufficient Tunisian talent has been attracted to dispense with nearly all foreign contract personnel."

Second, although the point is not explicitly emphasized, it is clear from Ashford's analysis that the status and support needed by a planning agency cannot be achieved merely by placing it in an appropriate location in the formal hierarchy of government. Waterston also recognizes that there is no magic in the location of a planning body. Yet in analyzing the weakness of Moroccan planning, he writes as follows:

Many of the problems encountered by the DCEP result from the fact that it had been placed too low in the organizational structure of the Government, where it had not the status and support to carry out the functions assigned to it. In consequence, the DCEP has often been compelled to work in isolation from the ministries, and on occasion, even from other parts of the Ministry of Economy and Finance. There is much to be said for raising the DCEP to a higher level to bring it as close as possible to the source of executive power. Until this is done, the DCEP will not be in position to function properly as a central planning body.[32]

In the light of the Moroccan political situation as described by Ashford, however, one might suppose that no significant change would take place even if the DCEP were moved into the private office of the Minister of Economy and Finance or straight into the palace chambers of King Hassan himself. The essence of a viable relation between a planning agency and political leaders is not heirarchic location. It is rather a relation of give-and-take in which the planning technicians must give such things as political commitment, behind-the-scenes participation in complex political negotiations, unending help in preparing political statements and speeches, and even, at times, assistance in election campaigns.

Third, Ashford's picture of Bourguiba's mobilization of support for Tunisian planning is a fine antidote for those who think that a national leader—even the charismatic leader of a single-party system—can get things done through the simple expedient of giving orders. With Ashford's help we see the slow tedious steps that are usually necessary in building political support for economic development. Before moving ahead vigorously on planning, Bourguiba first took steps to "free a third of the country's arable land from the deadening, inefficient control of religious foundations (habous)." At the same time he exploited "precedents for cooperative efforts in Islam." When the time came for more vigorous planning efforts, he put the new planning ministry under Ben Salah, who might otherwise have become a dangerous leftwing critic. He also went to great pains to maintain the confidence of private merchants and industrialists. Through the Economic and Social Council influential Tunisians from many divergent groups were brought together to consider the details of the plan. Labor

[32] Waterston, *Planning in Morocco*, p. 47.

and business organizations were encouraged to formulate proposals for inclusion in the plan. The Neo-Destour party set up study commissions throughout the country to take part in the planning process. It organized an "intensive program of indoctrination and persuasion" throughout the country and guided the plan through study by five subcommissions of the National Assembly. The result has been a development program far better articulated and far more widely supported than could possibly be produced by the "palace guard" in Morocco.

Yet one could scarcely describe the rationality of Bourguiba's approach to consensus-building as one that has been squarely based on economic desirability or has produced a "clear and consistent development policy." Both desirability and consistency have been repeatedly compromised in the interests of feasibility. Ceaseless bargaining and successive compromises have entered into both the formulation of goals and their implementation. Only thus is it possible to build the intricate coalition network and the web of unarticulated understandings that comprise the "activation base" [33] of planned economic development. Only thus is it possible to achieve the broader rationality that interweaves consideration of desirability, feasibility, and consistency into a truly optimal pattern of growth.[34]

BERTRAM M. GROSS

Syracuse, New York
Summer 1965

[33] The concept of "activation base," along with that of "activation mix," is set forth in general theory terms in Bertram M. Gross, *Activating National Plans,* Occasional Paper, Comparative Administration Group (American Society for Public Administration, 1964).

[34] The interrelation between desirability, feasibility, consistency, and optimal decision-making are set forth by Saul Katz in *A Systems Approach to Development Administration,* Special Series in Development Administration, Paper No. 6 (Comparative Administration Group, American Society for Public Administration, 1965). In a more theoretical form, together with a sharp distinction between "narrow" and "broad" rationality, a similar point of view is outlined in the section "The Action Concept of Rationality" in "Rationality: Satisfactory Action Patterns," Chap. 28, Gross, *The Managing of Organizations,* pp. 746–49.

Where Planning Begins

The widely accepted notion that economic planning is a natural sequel to the nationalist revolutions of Africa and Asia is quite misleading. A fundamental lesson to be drawn from our experience with foreign aid and other development activities is that political revolution does not necessarily produce social revolution. Entrenched groups and vested interests are as prevalent in the developing nation as in the more advanced nation. Given a generally less articulate populace and a highly centralized political system, the developing nation is probably more easily manipulated by influential groups than the more highly developed nation. Although ease of manipulation may greatly facilitate planned development or prevent serious obstacles, most leaders have exhibited caution, if not apprehension, over comprehensive planned change.

Unfortunately the American observer tends to equate political and economic radicalism, despite the evidence from our own history that demonstrates how easily these values may be dissociated in political life. The American public has been exposed to the skillfully designed propaganda of colonial powers, who have played on popular fears of Communist influence to retard the nationalist movements of Africa. While it is true that most nationalist leaders subscribe to some variety of socialism, it also is true that each has fashioned socialist principles to his needs. Without examining the political characteristics of the country concerned, one has no idea where such principles may lead or how they may be applied, if at all. Further, national planning is generally a consequence of socialist thought, but there are certainly as many different kinds of plans

1

in the non-Western world as there are different kinds of socialists. The most enlightened and moderate of British socialists would find Bourguiba's "Destourian socialism" very mild indeed. There are also several emergent countries, including Morocco, which have engaged in national planning with no doctrinaire presuppositions.

The personal predilections of nationalist leaders aside for the moment, there are probably three circumstances compelling them to accept some form of national planning.

First is the range of imponderable problems such as demographic growth, land erosion, slum dwellings, industrial unemployment, and many other complex and costly needs. A poor country that must provide fifty thousand jobs every year or that sees several hundred thousand acres of topsoil washed away with each rainy season simply must plan on a large scale. There are few solutions open to the half-sick, half-employed, half-literate citizen acting in isolation. A millennium of fairly indulgent use of resources under historic empires followed by a century or so of colonial exploitation of the most easily developed and marketed resources leaves little of immediate promise for individual development. The physical problems of the developing country mean that either the leaders plan on a reasonably ambitious scale or they permit themselves to be engulfed in the tide of misery and chaos resulting from inaction.

The second circumstance requiring national planning is the new nation's dependence on foreign assistance, both private and public. An American firm or the American government is unlikely to invest or loan huge sums without some knowledge of such things as the investment proposal, how long before the project will begin to pay for itself, and how the project fits into other needs and plans of the country. In some ways the private firm is even more exacting than national or international agencies, which have some funds for investment in infrastructure and for emergencies. The private investor wants to have a reasonably stable currency, developed banking institutions, systems of communication and transportation, to mention only a few conditions. The scale of the new nation's problems demands massive aid, and massive aid is not forthcoming without planning.

Probably the least important circumstance affecting the demand for planning is popular pressure. The Western image of the seething crowd forcing leaders to submit to excessive popular demands is only partly correct. Once the generally apathetic, discouraged masses of the developing nation are driven to violence to express their needs, it may well be too late to engage in planning. Naturally there is considerable sentiment in favor of national planning and control among educated elements in most emergent countries, but the informed represent a tiny minority and may be without influence. The alternatives are more realistically phrased when one realizes that it is not a choice between a set of values and planning but between chaos and planning. The new nation may be so late in turning to the problems of national planning that there will be little chance of production ever overcoming consumption. These are the situations of desperation that threaten Asian countries more than Africa and the Middle East. They manifest themselves in bloodshed and violence and are more costly than the most wild-eyed scheme of an inexperienced planning agency in a newly independent nation.

Once the necessity of national planning is acknowledged, the political problems created by planning are more intelligible. In practice, planning has had much less to do with doctrine or even pressing needs than with the decision-making capacity of the leaders and political forces of the various developing countries. Doctrine may be a source of motivational energy once a plan is being implemented, but it means relatively little in its commonly accepted sense of ultimate values in a non-Western political system. The reason for this is fairly clear. Nationalists have no shortage of ultimate values, and the creation of the nation is their overpowering goal. Their *raison d'être* has been forged in years of bitter conflict with colonial power. Indeed, the nationalist rationale may be so rigidly applied and so conceptually unimaginative that planning is handicapped. Confronted with the necessity of planning, the nationalists may become their own most serious obstacle. There is evidence for this conclusion in the experience of the North African planning agencies.

There are primarily three ways in which the nationalist political heritage may prove inappropriate to the needs of planning. First, every nationalist movement accumulates a long history of personal feuds and obligations during the struggle for independence. As will be seen in the Moroccan and Tunisian cases, the first years of independence are busy paying off old scores and old friends and consolidating one's power. Neither activity is conducive to objective, long-term planning. The nationalist movements are not nearly as cohesive as they appeared under the disciplinary effects of colonial oppression.[1] During the liberation struggle large sums are spent and many respected individuals give fortunes. Such persons are not likely to welcome a vigorous program to redistribute wealth or force savings once independence is achieved. Moreover, even the most fervent nationalists find themselves dependent on their colonial tutor in many ways, including reliance on colonial monetary supports and technical assistance. In North Africa the availability of French capital and talent has to some extent been dependent on preserving colonial privileges and attachments that conflict with long-range economic development.

Second, the governments of the developing nations are almost always organizationally unsuited to the needs of planning. There are several reasons for the organizational inadequacy. The highly centralized colonial governing pattern is generally accepted uncritically. In the Moroccan and Tunisian cases bureaucratic centralization has been particularly severe because of French administrative practice and the unusually close relation between the North African and French economies. For many years the large French populations of North Africa never imagined economic development apart from the Metropole. Algeria, of course, was treated as literally part of France, while both Morocco and Tunisia received aid and supervision from the *Commissariat du Plan* and the Office of European Economic Cooperation (OEEC). The North Africans have inherited the incredibly complex procedures of French financial services as they were once implanted to serve the needs of Paris. The Moroccan Ministry of Finance, for example, has remained one of the major obstacles to planning in that country, even though the planning agency was for many years in the same ministry.

Another contributing factor is the limited organizational experience of the nationalists themselves, who have almost no background in operating agencies concerned with intricate detail over long time periods. Further, the nationalists seldom have the kind of organization at the grassroots that is suited to the collection of information or supervision of diverse activity. The nationalist organization is designed to engage in mass activity and to utilize a self-justifying, uniform kind of activity. More attention will be given below to Bourguiba's efforts to convert the Neo-Destour organization to developmental needs. His entire reputation has been staked on such a conversion, and it is doubtful if any less forceful a figure than *le grand combattant* could have accomplished as much. In Morocco neither the nationalist party, the Istiqlal, nor the monarchy has been able or willing to accept comparable risk.

The third handicap of national planning in the developing country is psychological. Compared to our studies of political psychology in advanced societies, knowledge of the non-Westerner's attitudes toward government is very limited.[2] Nevertheless, useful insight can be found in comparing the intellectual framework of planning and nationalist politics. Nationalism concerns both mass identification and ultimate values.[3] The nationalist politician aims at uniting his people around a single imperative of self-evident importance and great persuasiveness. His appeal is emotional and affective. The psychological orientation compatible with long-range national planning, on the other hand, is almost the converse. Planning requires assigning priorities and concrete meanings to ultimate values. Specific choices having discernible individual and group impact must be made. The discipline and perseverance of the nationalist mode of action weakens when forced to articulate its ultimate values in an operational situation. The tasks of nation-building are neither dramatic nor inspiring, nor can anyone promise the same chance of fulfillment allotted to the determined nationalist. Failure in planning brings disgrace rather than martyrdom.

In many ways the nationalist leaders are singularly unsuited to the developmental phase of their countries' growth. They are not used to the methods of administrative accountability and allocation required by planning. They are often reluctant to be associated too closely with any specific group. Like their Western counterparts, nationalist figures dislike making concrete choices, but the Westerner seldom uses uncertainty and ambiguity as a method of governing. The advanced state of the industrial nation entails the application of a more complex way of thinking about the world. The newly installed nationalist does not bring nearly as complex cognitive structures to his tasks. His work in the nationalist movement has not forced him to articulate and reconcile his attitudes, and his comparatively simple society does not require such attention and analysis from its participants. As a political problem, planning is probably most intriguing as a revealing focus for the study of nationalist psychology under stress.

Because this inquiry is particularly concerned with the implications of planning for more diverse, increased participation, the role of the government has crucial importance. Essentially, the government is asking citizens to become more active, and is indeed placing new resources and income at their disposal. The economic success of the plan may depend on how successfully the government can reinvest as income grows. But the economic version of participation by a population with increased influence on the development process is vastly simplified. Not only does the citizen hopefully have more income and goods, but he also knows more about government. [As planning advances, he learns how to deal with officials rather than submit to or deceive them.] His entire cognitive world grows as he finds that governmental policies may in fact affect conditions for his family, his children's opportunities and his own security. [Thus, planning involves not only getting the citizen to do different things, but also his understanding of how new behavior holds together.] Imperfect as his understanding may be, it represents an important new source of influence in the developing country, which nationalist leadership is frequently reluctant to accommodate. In fact, vigorous planners, as in the Tunisian case, may not have perceived the individual transformation that their efforts were bringing about.

The foregoing observations on the historical, organizational, and psychological hazards of long-term national planning will be elaborated in the following sections of the essay. The first two sections will deal with the background of planning in both Morocco and Tunisia. In many ways these sections will also be an evaluation of the political system of each country and its effectiveness as the planning instrument. In the developing country the decision to undertake planning is probably the most difficult step in the whole planning process. The decision brings into focus all the planning hazards mentioned above, and may often become a turning point in the political development of the newly created state. The background sections will be followed with two sections devoted to the political implications of planning and how the plan relates to political interests in each country. The concluding section will put forward some suggestions as to how increasing commitment to planned change will affect political development in Morocco, Tunisia, and in the non-Western countries generally.

Political Forces in the Commitment to Planning

How the nation makes the decision to plan tells a good deal about how political forces are managed, and how, in turn, the political system might cope with new political forces set in motion by developmental successes. While it must be acknowledged that Morocco is on the whole a more traditional society than Tunisia, the Moroccan experience vividly demonstrates how difficult it has been to relate planning to political forces in even a rudimentary manner. The problem is not to arrive at a perfect solution to the political life that will inevitably stem from the decisions to be made in planning and from the more influential citizen who will eventually emerge as implementation takes place. Although the decision to plan and the planning process are administratively discrete acts, they are not clearly differentiated in the mind of the citizen and probably not considered separately by leadership. For this reason, the following treatment may to some extent blur the continuing role of leader and citizen in planning. However, it makes possible a description of how participation changed in the two societies once very different initial strategies for national reconstruction were selected.

Effective planning and development involve not only the design for national reconstruction but also the integration of a variety of new behavior. The traditionally oriented system has certain advantages in making such a transition, most often described by the universalistic value system supporting traditional regimes. Experience in Africa has suggested that transferral of such values to a new social system is extremely difficult. The influence of Islam and the historic role of the monarch gave Morocco such an advantage, but

7

it has been extremely difficult to attach new behavior to these values. Rather than serving as a widely accepted focus for resolving differences and introducing new social goals, Moroccan values have tended to become a rigid framework, and their appeal has been transformed into a demand for obedience to the established authority. Rather than use Moroccan beliefs as the basis for accommodating more diverse behavior in a single value system, popular beliefs have been used to exclude and manipulate forces considered a threat to the political system, thereby eliminating them from the government and, to that extent, depriving the government of many articulate and talented leaders. Thus, traditional values, in becoming a defense for the *status quo,* cannot be applied to the more delicate task of implementing a plan and introducing new behavior.

The steady deterioration of planning activity in Morocco contrasts sharply with the growing emphasis and success of planning in Tunisia, which is much less generously endowed. As pointed out below, the commitment to planning was not without threat to the Neo-Destour, significantly renamed the Constitutionalist (Destourian) Socialist party in October 1964. But the mobilization regime finds its justification in its ability to deliver and to perform. In a sense, values are directly consumed in a traditional society in order to find gratification, but in the single-party states of Africa, for example, values tend to be accepted for their instrumental quality. For this reason, it is much easier for the Neo-Destour to justify new behavior and to relate social change to principles that have guided the party since its inception. The party becomes an institution to create new kinds of influence and, in so doing, to make sure that new centers of power are aligned with the party. The difficulty of achieving such a balance explains the reluctance of many Neo-Destour leaders to favor active planning. The commitment to planning in Tunisia was, in fact, associated with the leaders' realization that the party was stagnating and that failing to advocate new achievements for Tunisian society sacrificed the rationale for party influence and power.

MOROCCO: NATIONALIST DISINTEGRATION AND POLITICAL INDECISION

In Morocco there was only desultory recognition of the need to engage in planning over the first year of independence. Although there were some vigorous leaders advocating national planning, the government was badly divided over policies and priorities. The nationalist movement soon found itself confronted with several minor parties, while the predominant, traditionally inclined elements within the Istiqlal found it increasingly difficult to accommodate the progressive preoccupations of a growing radical faction. The monarch, the late Mohammed V, tended to govern by a process of allowing all groups to exhaust themselves in discussion, while using makeshift interim arrangements to operate the government. While this was a commendably tolerant procedure, it could not operate effectively without some institutional framework to place responsibility and minimize intrigue.

Moroccan politicians had great difficulty in coming to grips with the concrete issues of their country's future. To the uncertainties of the governing process were added the factionalism of the multiparty system and the distractions of a growing irredentist movement under the Istiqlal leader, Allal Al-Fassi. Moreover, the Protectorate administrative structure, burdensome and top-heavy as it might be, was designed to avoid disaster rather than initiate change. The French bureaucracy at home and overseas had long acted as the country's managerial agent. There were many offices from Protectorate days that ostensibly provided the coordination a planning agency hopefully brings to a country's economic life. Only with time did the Moroccan leaders realize that the security of these offices depended on accepting the colonial presuppositions and purposes for which they were first erected.

Under the French Protectorate Morocco had been developed by the intricate mosaic of private, public, and semipublic corporations much like those found in France. The first Resident General, Marshal Lyautey, set a precedent for planned development by setting aside Morocco's rich phosphate deposits as a state monopoly in 1923. A few years later a governmental agency was created to attract mining companies for the exploitation of lead, manganese, zinc, and other mineral deposits. However, neither agency was used with the imagination needed to promote the economy as a whole. The Sherifian Phosphate Office accumulated large reserves that could not be used in other sectors of the economy. The profitable businesses that its activity assures were judiciously doled out to French firms. The mining agency, the Office for Research and Participation in Mining (*Bureau de Recherches et de Participation Minières*), was reportedly used to defray the expenses of private firms without exacting appropriate guarantees from the firms.

French budgetary procedures contain a deceptive element of planned organization. The budget is normally presented in two parts: the ordinary, or operating, budget and the equipment, or capital, budget. In practice the French have negated this very logical division of funds by allowing some capital funds to be used for operating expenses, and by including costs that might be more reasonably classified as capital investment in the operating budget. Each ministry prepares a public works program, a practice that was adopted by the Moroccan services and directories in 1944. The program is approved piecemeal as the ministry concerned can convince the government, or can smuggle parts of the program into either of the two budgets. Needless to say, the orderliness of this procedure is more apparent than real. Integrated development programs are almost impossible, and interministry feuding can have paralytic effects.

The French economic reforms of 1946 failed to dislodge an entrenched Protectorate administration. The Parisian *Commissariat Général du Plan* was quite rightly regarded by most Protectorate officials as too heavily staffed with persons whose ideas, political and otherwise, might upset the Protectorate and who might mingle too freely with the growing numbers of nationalist politicians. All three North African countries were excluded from the French ten-year plan (1947–1956). Morocco proceeded to work from compilations of ministerial public works programs, while receiving French investment funds.

Ultra-conservative French elements in North Africa probably found their worst fears confirmed when the Marshall Plan finally brought about closer supervision of investment and planning in North Africa. Since Franklin D. Roosevelt's famous meeting with Mohammed V, the United States has been regarded by conservatives as a political and economic threat to French hegemony in the area. Under the Marshall Plan two modernization and investment programs were devised for Morocco, using the French ten-year plan as a model. The first was to run from 1949 to 1952 and was later extended to 1953, while the second operated from 1954 to 1957.[1] Under the circumstances the first plan was largely an amalgamation of existing schemes, but the second plan surveyed Moroccan needs and Protectorate policy more critically.

For the second plan the first Moroccan Planning Office (*Bureau du Plan*) was established, first in the Department of Agriculture and later under the secretary general of the Protectorate, the central coordinating official for the entire government. The Planning Office was run by a French civil servant and several clerks, who submitted their investment proposals to a study group established for all North Africa. The report of this group constituted the plan as it was submitted to the French planning agency and later to the French parliament. It is interesting to note that the second Protectorate plan marks the beginning of over-all economic policy formation. The report was openly critical of the near total neglect by the government of the traditional agricultural sector of the economy, while it built large-scale irrigation schemes and machinery centers that did little to help the Moroccan peasant. The report also noted the disruptive effect of administrative infighting in the Moroccan government and the Protectorate's failure to enlist the collaboration of the Moroccans in economic development.[2] The document must have alarmed the Protectorate regime, which shared the extremely conservative reaction throughout the Maghrib as French politics swung to the right over the past decade.

Compared to many of the more recently independent countries, Morocco had considerable experience in national planning at the time of independence. Admittedly, this experience was largely under the supervision of French officials, many of whom left in 1956, but there were certainly individuals in the Moroccan ministries and Metropole agencies familiar with Moroccan developmental problems. Many of the economists connected with French planning agencies were of liberal, if not socialist, tendencies and as such were generally trusted by the nationalists. Thus, it is probably fair to evaluate Morocco as quite well off in terms of experienced personnel and cumulative developmental effort in 1956. The fact that the independent government largely ignored this experience and failed to build on previous planning efforts can be explained only by examining the politics of a liberated Morocco.

During the first months of independence the Planning Office remained attached to the secretary general's office. The Istiqlal was occupied with asserting its claims to positions in the cabinet, and many of its leaders were fully occupied with the negotiations to establish the new nation's international position. By late 1956 it became apparent to the Istiqlal that the King had no intention of giving ministerial power to his cabinet members. Key positions were filled with close personal friends of the monarch. The president of the cabinet or Council of Government could not make decisions without the King's authorization. The extremely centralized pattern of government also meant that the secretary general, whose position as personal aide to the King for the entire administration probably makes him more powerful than a minister, had no time to supervise the Planning Office.

On the Protectorate model, economic affairs were split among three ministries: Finance, Commerce and Industry, and Industrial Production and Mining. The consequent administrative tangles were further complicated by party divisions among the three ministers. Agriculture was initially placed in the hands of one of the major landholders of the Gharb plain. For reasons of political pride more than concern over the increasing economic disintegration of the country, the Istiqlal demanded more representation in the cabinet in the fall of 1956. Two changes were made at this time that would facilitate planned change and were no doubt partly inspired by the growing administrative chaos. The three ministries concerned with economic problems were assigned to a single "superministry" under the Istiqlal's Abderahim Bouabid. Public works and housing were also merged in one ministry under a bright young Istiqlal engineer, Mohammed Douiri. Agriculture was given to an esteemed elder of the Istiqlal, whose infirmities and nationalist preoccupations left little time for the office.

Bouabid was almost certainly the leading figure in the reorganization toward increased effectiveness in dealing with the country's sagging economy, and he remained the most outspoken exponent of national planning. Probably under conditions laid down by him during the cabinet reorganization, the Planning Office was moved to his ministry in November 1956, along with the statistical and publications services of the secretary general. Under Bouabid's direction plans were made for an expanded national planning agency. They were slow to materialize, partly because of the cumbersome practices of the Moroccan government and partly because of indecisive leadership. It should also be noted that the Moroccan concessions to party activity place certain limits on the dispatch with which controversial actions can be taken. In Tunisia Bourguiba prepares his people for the major changes in policy, but there are relatively few problems at the higher levels of government. Each procedure has advantages and disadvantages, which will be further discussed in the conclusion.

Bouabid's proposal for a Superior Planning Council (*Conseil Supérieur du Plan*) was contained in a law passed in June 1957.[3] The twenty-four members of the council included most of the cabinet, representatives of the National Consultative Assembly, three agricultural representatives, three union representatives, and one each for handicrafts, industry, and commerce. The outside representatives were selected by the three pressure groups for agriculture (*L'Union Marocaine d'Agriculture*), for labor (*L'Union Marocaine de Travail*), and for business (*L'Union Marocaine de l'Industrie, de Commerce et d'Artisanat*). The council was to be supported by a committee on finance and by a series of specialized commissions. The planning organization was almost identical to the French organization.[4] The new organization was completed in the fall of 1957 when a special division (*Division de la Coordination Economique et du Plan*) was created to prepare working papers, conduct research, and supervise the execution of the Superior Planning Council's decisions.

[Having gone through all the motions of serious planning, the Moroccan government simply failed to use the new agencies or to follow through with its announced intentions. This failure to use valuable human and organizational resources is characteristic of Moroccan politics and the explanation can be found only by viewing the developing political system broadly. The concessions made to Bouabid were in part to placate a political point of view and were typical of the relatively complex pattern of bargaining and compromise that has continually gone on in the higher levels of the Moroccan government. The ostensible maturity and impressive moderation of this activity is misleading because it has not led to effective decision-making. Morocco is sufficiently wealthy to permit this sort of indulgence, while Tunisia is not. The Moroccan people find themselves caught in an unproductive political pattern from which they cannot emerge.]

In 1958 good crops meant that there was relatively little rural unrest, but the poor year in 1959 plus increased economic problems resulting from capital withdrawal and currency reform contributed to the tribal revolts of late 1958. Morocco had not found means of relating the government to the needs and wishes of her people. Planning is not only erecting the semblance of economic order on paper but making decisions on the basis of such plans that will strike a compromise between the needs of economic growth and political stability. Although starting out with certain advantages in both resources and organization, the Moroccan planning activity has never been closely related to the political life of the country. The tightly centralized administration, the shortsightedness of parties and groups, and the extreme cautiousness of the Palace made effective action difficult. The tragedy is twofold, for Morocco did not only lose opportunities to make material progress at an early phase in her development, but she also lost the rare opportunities the new country has to build political confidence and relate her social needs to the political process in a convincing manner. The political costs are more difficult to calculate but very likely represent losses that no amount of funds can recover.

Almost nothing was done for two years. The Division for Economic Coordination and the Plan produced a biennial plan for the years 1958/1959,[5] which was largely an interim document compiled from existing uncoordinated plans from the various ministries. The Superior Planning Council did not meet, nor did the parties demand that it meet. The National Consultative Assembly held perfunctory debates on the biennial plan, but no substantial criticism was made. The more progressive political forces, centered around Bouabid, Ben Barka, the President of the National Consultative Assembly, and Mahjoub Ben Seddiq, the President of the Moroccan Labor Federation (*L'Union Marocaine du Travail* [UMT]), found themselves increasingly isolated in the government. Within the Istiqlal the progressive faction was viewed with skepticism, if not apprehension, by the nationalist elders. Some old-guard leaders were interested in reclaiming Morocco's historic empire,[6] while others were deeply committed to the conservative policies of Moroccan business and the Palace. In this situation the diversity and comparative wealth of Morocco could not be combined in a vigorous, unified approach to the country's future. Planning, as well as many other basic national problems, went unattended.

By 1959 relations between the urban, worker-based faction of the progressives and the conservative faction of the Palace and old-guard Istiqlal had become so poor that the Istiqlal split. In a letter to the King, Bouabid complained that the ministries could not become effective organizations unless the monarch were willing to delegate power.[7] There is good evidence that this was not a complaint solely of the left. Balafrej, an old-guard Istiqlal figure and one-time president of the cabinet, had taken office in 1958 only after noting that he had received "formal assurances" of the "necessary means to govern." [8] The crisis was momentarily resolved by allowing a highly regarded leader of the progressives, Abdallah Ibrahim, to become president of the cabinet without full powers (*à titre personnel*). His appointment raised hopes that planning and other basic economic matters would finally receive attention.

Many of the fundamental institutional structures for economic planning and investment were set up by Ibrahim and Bouabid during 1959. An Office for Industrial Research and Participation (*Bureau d'Etudes et de Participations Industrielles*) had been started in late 1957, but there had been no banking or currency measures to attract funds or to distinguish Moroccan banking institutions from their French superiors. In mid-1959 a National Bank for Economic Development (*Banque Nationale pour le Développement Economique*) was organized along with an industrial and commercial research group, the Moroccan Study and Industrial Coordination Company (*Société d'Etudes et de Coordination Industrielle Marocaine*). Bouabid also tried to redress Morocco's unfavorable trade balance and to exercise more control over commerce. The franc was devalued and Morocco established her own bank of issue, the *Banque du Maroc*, and a commercial exchange bank, the *Banque du Commerce Extérieur*. In agriculture some preliminary steps were made toward reform with the "Operation Plow," which consisted of mechanically plowing consolidated lands and distributing improved seed and fertilizer.[9] Impressive as these measures might be, they were made possible only by the near emergency situation in agriculture because of drought and the country's increasing economic plight. They were not part of a coordinated government scheme to attack selected problems basic to the Moroccan economy, nor did they receive the wholehearted support of the government.

Late in 1959 Bouabid assembled the long inactive Superior Planning Council and its fifteen specialized commissions. Each commission had received a note of "orientation" early in 1959, and work was supposed to be proceeding on the projected five-year plan for 1960–1964. It became apparent that each commission had become the instrument of the dominant interest it represented and that the projects were being designed with no consideration of financial or related needs of the economy. In his speech to the commissions Bouabid admitted that the country had not yet "undertaken planning in the rigorous sense of the term" and that previous efforts had been little more than consolidated investment budgets. He strongly criticized the commission's "complete indifference" to the problems of finance and stressed the need to use local materials and skill.[10]

For reasons that are still not entirely clear, the Ibrahim government was dismissed just before elections in May 1960. Mohammed V became the president of the cabinet, and his son, Moulay Hassan, the vice president. Since it was known that the monarch was reluctant to become directly involved in the operation of government, it is clear that this was a measure of the last resort after alternative cabinet arrangements had proved unfeasible. Relations between the Istiqlal and the party of the progressives, the National Union (L'Union National des Forces Populaires) became increasingly embittered as quarrels followed over the allegiance of workers, youth, and farmers. The local elections did not serve to clear the air, nor did the Palace undertake to realign the cabinet or other institutions in order to make the initial concession to local government more meaningful.[11]

Under the chairmanship of the Prince, now King Moulay Hassan II, the Superior Planning Council met to discuss the five-year plan in August 1960. The minutes of the meetings make clear how divided the council's members were and how totally lacking the plan was in a central concept or purpose. Even the Istiqlal minister who replaced Bouabid was not fully in accord with the Prince. In Douiri's opening statement he virtually admitted that the plan had not yet been evaluated for its impact on the economy as a whole and confessed that more effective planning would be impossible unless the Division of Economic Coordination and Planning were given real powers.[12] Since he was minister of national economy, the revelation suggests that the internal operation of the government had not changed noticeably from the confused months following independence.

The most outspoken rejection came from the labor representatives. Their complaints, however, were directed more against the Prince and their political rivals than against the plan. The representatives of the landowners and of business made pleas for their particular interests, too. The meeting closed with another speech from the Prince that served to confuse the proceedings by introducing a proposal for an arms industry, which was not mentioned in the plan, and making suggestions on possible sources of foreign capital that were also new. The meeting ended arbitrarily and the council has not been convened since. Without further discussion the five-year plan was later approved by the King and issued as a law.[13]

The political implications of the five-year plan will be discussed further below, but it is important to note how planning activity deteriorated as the internal politics became more bitter. No influential figure or group could afford to ignore the national planning effort, but neither could such figures or groups agree. By the time the country had prepared a plan, which is not original in its concepts or goals, political forces had diverged so greatly that it was almost impossible to give the plan any meaning in the internal political life of the country. The Istiqlal managed to give the plan sufficient lip service to defend the Istiqlal ministers associated with it, but the party found it difficult to display any enthusiasm for economic reforms. The National Union, whose leaders actually conceived the plan, became its most vociferous critic. The monarchy failed to rally popular support for the plan, while discouraging more articulate political groups by arbitrarily imposing favored projects and denying basic powers to the planning agency. The promising beginnings of the Moroccan planning effort were dissipated in political bickering and intrigue.

TUNISIA: NATIONALIST SOLIDARITY AND POLITICAL PROCRASTINATION

The decision to undertake comprehensive planning in Tunisia is much less the product of divergent political forces than is the case in Morocco. Largely because of President Bourguiba's personal forcefulness a single-party system has been maintained. While there are certainly a variety of points of view within the Neo-Destour, and some negligible centers of political opposition in Tunis, very little is done without the President's final approval. The character of Tunisian leadership, and the requirements of the single-party system, mean that new ideas and compelling goals are constantly being used to sustain discipline and monopolize the popular imagination. While it is correct that Tunisia has accomplished more in national planning and in many other fields than Morocco, there are very clearly certain limitations to personalized politics.

Two factors placing irremovable limits on Tunisian economic reform should be mentioned first. The country is much poorer than Morocco, with a per capita income of about $120 a year, or about two-thirds of Morocco's per capita wealth. This has meant that Tunisia is much more dependent on the privileges obtained from economic submission to France and on the monetary stability derived from the franc zone. At the same time Tunisia has been more directly involved in the Algerian war than Morocco, whose effort was minor during the early years of the revolution and was later concentrated in a fairly remote region. The Algerians have always been present in large numbers in Tunisia, and since 1957 they have had extensive rights in large areas of the country. This combination of factors placed Tunisia in a more delicate situation than Morocco.

A country's capacity to understand the requirements and the advantages of planning depends in part on the pervasiveness of the colonial power's impact. While large parts of Morocco were relatively untouched by the Protectorate in the short span of one generation, Tunisia has been much more widely and more deeply affected by three generations of French occupation. Although bureaucratic habits may be more deeply ingrained, and cultural imperialism, so central to the French colonial concept, may have left deeper marks in Tunisian life, the higher degree of mastery of Western ideas has probably given Tunisians a greater capacity to criticize French ideas and to manipulate Western notions to the country's needs. Quite clearly Tunisia did not display Morocco's unfamiliarity with planning, and an influential segment of the population presented well-developed concepts of planning immediately after independence. Few Moroccan groups have as clear or original ideas on the role of planning in the developing country.

Although French interests were more limited in Tunisia than in Morocco, the governmental structure had longer to develop and the French *présence* had time to spread over more of the country. Before the turn of the century the secretary general of the government had been dissolved in favor of specialized ministerial departments. A system of regional representation including a Tunisian minority was established in 1922, and the Grand Council of Tunisia had special commissions to suggest public works projects and possible sources of revenue for local projects.[14] These concessions were certainly not disinterested or aimed at creating self-government for the Tunisian Protectorate, but they did provide experience, which helps account for the relatively sophisticated approach to planning in Tunisia.

Like Morocco, Tunisia's needs were examined under the postwar planning activities of France and the Marshall Plan. As in the rest of the Maghrib, the plans were strongly influenced by the needs of the French population, especially the settlers and corporate farms, whose interests were concentrated in the north. Two four-year plans were made, one for 1948–52 and another for 1953–57. Although consultative commissions were organized, the center and south were represented only by persons from Sfax and Sousse, the two major cities of Tunisia's eastern coastline.[15] As in Morocco, the first plan concentrated on repairing the damage of the war and allocated seventy million dollars to the development of the lower Mejerda Valley, a project the Tunisian government has continued on an expanded scale. The second plan put more stress on agricultural improvement, but the bulk of the funds were allocated to the more prosperous, French-controlled regions in the north.

The initial geographical disparities of French planning had a deep effect on the Tunisian nationalists. Unlike the Istiqlal, which was practically confined to the agriculturally rich areas before independence, the Neo-Destour had strong support from the center and south. In the central coastal plains, known as the Sahel, the party had historic roots and Bourguiba himself came from a small town south of Sousse. The Sousse region is still a Neo-Destour stronghold. Farther south, Tunisia's active trade union movement had its foundations in the phosphate industry, which spread from inland mines around Ghafsa to the port of Sfax. The Tunisian labor movement, which has much earlier origins than the Moroccan

UMT, had a key nationalist organization immediately after the war under the vigorous leadership of Farhat Hached.

The more even dispersion of nationalist influence in Tunisia has had important effects on the development of the Neo-Destour since independence, especially on planning activity. There has never been any doubt of the need to assist the areas neglected under the Protectorate. Further, the neglected areas had influential representation in the party and in the unions. Because of the labor organization's activity in the south, Tunisian workers were never as preoccupied with a single industrial concentration like Casablanca. Therefore, it was possible to get labor support for regional development, and union leaders were aware of the hardships of life in Tunisia's remote provinces. While Moroccan politicians have certainly been aware of the regional differences of their country, they were not conditioned to the need for national economic integration to nearly the same degree as the Tunisians.

The Tunisian approach to planning since independence differs greatly from the Moroccan experience. Although Bourguiba had to contend with an aging Bey of doubtful nationalist loyalty, he was the unchallenged leader of the party and the country. In the first interim government, in which Bourguiba did not participate, economic affairs were left largely in the hands of respected merchant and business families. In late 1955 Bourguiba was fully occupied repelling Salah Ben Youssef's attack on his policies. He emerged victorious at the Sfax Congress of November 1955, where first mention appears of the need to engage in national planning. Unlike the Istiqlal congress of this period, which only agreed on an innocuous motion concerning the need for economic improvement and social justice, the Neo-Destour Congress specifically endorsed planning. The motion on economic affairs "urged the elaboration of a national program of economic expansion and social progress," and the party's Political Bureau was explicitly charged with designing such a program.[16]

Although Bourguiba enjoyed undisputed preeminence among the nationalist forces in Tunisia, there were still wide differences of opinion concerning the country's future. His tactic of bargaining for gradual concessions from the French was made possible by the support he received from the influential Tunisian *bourgeoisie* of the large towns. At the same time, he had to guard against the creation

of a left-wing Arabist or socialist party. The Arabist threat was removed with Ben Youssef's defeat, but the socialist appeal was strong
in union ranks. With ample support from American unions, the
General Union of Tunisian Workers (*L'Union Générale des Travailleurs Tunisiennes*) had developed a strong organization and
imaginative leadership. The UGTT's Secretary General, Ahmed
Ben Salah, advocated a distinctly socialist line of economic development and felt that the workers were entitled to special recognition
for their sacrifices on behalf of the Neo-Destour. His views were all
the more conspicuous because of Bourguiba's lack of interest in
economic affairs and distrust of doctrine of any kind, which was
basically incompatible with his style of leadership.

There were certainly influential groups pressing for comprehensive planning immediately after independence, but the concentrated
effort needed for effective planning was difficult in the rush of post-
independence events. The country's first concern was financial stability, and Bourguiba, who became premier before creating the
office of president, selected Hedi Nouira for the post of finance
minister. Nouira supervised this ministry until becoming director of
the national bank (*Banque Centrale*). The minister of economic
affairs in the first government was from a wealthy Tunisian family
and president of the merchants' association. Relying on conservative Tunisians and French support, Bourguiba could not risk the
loss of confidence that might result from interfering too strenuously
in the economy. Further, the premier was busy planning religious
reforms in order to free a third of the country's arable land from
the deadening, inefficient control of religious foundations (*habous*).
He was also preparing to remove the Bey and establish a constitutional regime with himself as president. Although Bourguiba gave
qualified approval to planning in his speech to the Constituent Assembly in April 1956, he took no action.

Preoccupied with these maneuvers, Bourguiba lost his grip on
the labor movement, and the UGTT congress of September 1956
openly challenged his policies. Central to the congress' report was
the establishment of a powerful planning agency and a variety of
new controls on the economy. The report was pointedly addressed
to those who "distrust improvisation" and wish to "regard the future
lucidly." [17] Bourguiba's government was openly charged with finding "endless pretexts to put off the moment when it might conse-

crate itself" and with having a "certain ignorance of the power of economic and social forces." The remnants of French planning activity that were part of the premier's office were described as "small and derisory." The planning proposal is very close to the position created for Ben Salah five years after his critical report was issued. The 1956 proposal called for a first vice president for policy matters and a second vice president for planning, who would coordinate the Ministeries of Agriculture, Public Works, Finance, Industry and Commerce, Education, Public Health, and Postal Services. The ambitiousness of the suggestion is indicative of the proponent's inexperience as well as his energy.

Bourguiba was not prepared to undertake such an ambitious proposal in late 1956, much less to organize another office that might threaten his own before the Bey's position had been dissolved. The result of the crisis was a scission of the UGTT between factions under Ben Salah and Tilili, secretary of the union until removed in 1963 for resisting party policy.[18] The split was not healed until late 1957. By then the Bey had been removed, and Ben Salah had agreed to take the Ministry of Public Health and Labor, where he could maintain contact with the workers and also use his organizational skill to the nation's advantage. However, Bourguiba, by then President of the Republic, is much too capable a politician to allow an opponent's appeal to go unheeded. Early in 1958 the National Planning Council was established, quite possibly as part of the compromise to end the trade union quarrel and reconcile Ben Salah to his new post.

Although the Tunisian planning agency differs from the Moroccan agency in that there was identifiable demand for its creation and a reasonably precise proposal for its role, it did not become an important group. There are several reasons for this. Tunisia became increasingly embroiled in the Algerian revolution in 1957, and the Sakiet-Sidi-Youssef attack heightened the sense of crisis in the country. There are more profound reasons, however, that rest more squarely on the character of the single-party system that Bourguiba so masterfully constructed over thirty years. Bourguiba enjoys the detail and complexity of planning even less than Mohammed V. While he has welcomed French advocates of planning,[19] he has been interested in them more for the moving ideas they might provide and, of course, their total dependence on his judgment as to when to make critical decisions. The effectiveness of the single-party system should not be underestimated, but its advantages cannot be manifested unless such decisions are made. Bourguiba could not permit them to be made in an open assembly where he might appear as simply a moderator. If the bargaining and groundwork for major decisions had to be carried on under cover, then some appropriate device was needed to explain delay and distract critics. The National Planning Council was such an agency.

The law establishing the council acknowledged the aims of planning much more clearly than the similar Moroccan law. The council was to fix economic goals, elaborate programs to achieve them, decide on priorities and rates of growth, propose which sectors should receive attention and how funds might be obtained, and suggest measures to stimulate private initiative as well.[20] The council was composed of key members of the President's office, the ministers concerned with economic and social affairs, two representatives of the National Assembly, and four representatives of national organizations—labor, commerce, agriculture, and banking. By omitting discussion of general goals or doctrine at the council's first meeting, Bourguiba reassured those elements who might consider the new agency an approval of Ben Salah's 1956 report. The President noted that the plan would not eliminate or obstruct private initiative. He suggested that it start with more promising projects and did not mention the more controversial commercial and industrial sectors.

Although the new planning agency was very likely a factor in the reconciliation of Ahmed Ben Salah and the President, like the Moroccan planning agency, it could do very little until the interested groups were prepared to cooperate. The process of establishing the confidence of influential Tunisians constitutes a revealing comparison with the Moroccan experience. In Morocco the Superior Planning Council was the expression of a political stalemate. The progressives placed great hopes on planning but had neither the influence with the Palace nor the informed body of followers to make planning activities acceptable. The groups opposed to more controlled economic life could achieve their purposes through inaction and obstruction. Tunisian officials, too, were well aware that there were strong backers for the *status quo* in their country. However, they were able to mobilize opinion and create an efficient planning group in less time.

Bourguiba is an experienced infighter. His experience is displayed in his willingness to forego combat until the most advantageous moment and in his skill in keeping his opponents separated. While there is no evidence that he looked upon the National Planning Council as anything more than a political concession to progressive critics in 1958, it became the bulwark of his policy in 1961. To understand the change of view during this period, it is necessary to note the transformation of the Neo-Destour that the President created in the interim. Certainly he was aware of the growing economic misery of his country, but he also became increasingly aware that the small entrepreneur and merchant was a greater threat to party hegemony than the new urban radicals he pacified with the planning agency. The exact sequence of his thought is not clear, but the process of his active conversion to planning may be followed and its results identified.

Perhaps the turning point came in the fall of 1958, when Bourguiba encountered resistance to his plan for reorganizing the party. He had planned to replace the provincial committees, consisting largely of local party elders and influential citizens, with *délégués,* or centrally appointed officials.[21] The objections were lodged so effectively that the Congress was postponed until the spring of 1959, by which time the party had managed to pacify or remove the centers of resistance. The incident very likely served to alert the President to the extremely conservative and parochial views of the party militants. If the party became sufficiently localized, the single-party structure would collapse and the President's authority would be compromised. Although a diffusion of power might be desirable for the development of a more democratic regime, the conservative outlook of most provincial and cell committees outside Tunis meant that the party organization, the most important force in Tunisia, would probably not respond to the needs of planned economic growth.[22]

Within the government there were at least three events paving the way for increased planning. These experiences may have convinced Bourguiba that more centralized planning would not endanger his position and might even enhance it. As minister of public health and labor, Ahmed Ben Salah was both loyal and effective. His comprehensive and energetic attack on Tunisia's public health problems could not help but impress others. As a result of poor harvests in 1957, Tunisia also began to accept surplus American wheat under emergency provisions. The food was distributed to pay for labor on public works projects, whose value as centers of indoctrination, education, and economic development was soon apparent to the Tunisians.[23] Further, the distribution and accounting procedures may have demonstrated to more skeptical officials how a nationally organized scheme for local improvement might be administered. Lastly, the Ministry of Education, under one of Bourguiba's most trusted colleagues, Mesadi, produced a ten-year plan for education in 1958.[24] The plan was further evidence of the advantages of planning, and may very well have set officials in other ministries to thinking about possibilities and needs in their sectors.

These internal events, and possibly others, combined with the continuing crisis in Algeria to make the appeal of the "economic battle" more attractive. Without Morocco's wealth the Tunisians could not adopt the most elementary institutional reforms for economic development without reasonable certainty of popular support. Still omitting the more controversial sectors of commerce and industry, Bourguiba began injecting in his speeches comments about the need to mobilize popular energies in developing the countryside and of the benefits to be had from centrally directed reforms in education, health, public housing, and land reform. During the party's Sousse Congress and the campaign for the National Assembly elections in late 1959, Bourguiba stressed these concrete benefits of governmental intervention in social and economic affairs, but he did not publicly advocate more energetic planning.[25]

Given the foregoing predisposing factors, it is surprising that the Tunisians delayed as long as they did. There was very little increase in agitation for central planning in 1960, although the national organizations affiliated with the Neo-Destour continue to discuss it at their congresses. It appears that Bourguiba might have been seeking the compromise among auxiliary organizations that commonly precedes public discussion. The pattern of gradually expanding the circle of discussion as the inner, more powerful circles of party and government agree to reforms has been followed before in Tunisia and is standard single-party practice. Limited agreement among power centers is required before less easily manipulated forces are aroused.

The first public bid for increased planning came from the unions in their Eighth National Congress of April 1960. While the UGTT has always maintained that it is not subordinate to the Neo-Destour, it has seldom disagreed publicly with the party and is amply represented on high party committees. As the report stated, the union has always regarded the Neo-Destour as "its 'socialist' party," adhering to governmental policy by conviction while maintaining "material and moral independence." [26] While there are probably few party militants outside the unions who would accept this interpretation of either the party or the union, it has been a convenient device to preserve the solidarity of the single-party system. This does not mean that the union has been forbidden to criticize, or even to differ with, the government.

Thus, the report noted that the UGTT still prefers "an economic system based on cooperation and popular association of investment funds assuring the socialization of the means of production." The report also conceded that the capitalist-inspired groups of businessmen and landowners had begun to recognize the country's proletarian base and to subscribe to more progressive policies. However, the UGTT still had certain reservations on economic policy, which were published separately from the report. In a brochure entitled *On the Difficult Road to Development* the union spokesman noted that the National Planning Council had "unhappily" not met since its creation in 1958.[27] It also mentioned that the special funds promised for the development of the central and southern regions had not been forthcoming. The paper ended by stressing planning as the sole solution to Tunisia's problems. Such a plan must include all sectors of the economy for at least a decade. The plan must also be administered directly under the authority of the President and govern the policies of the various ministries.

The document reveals how severe the internal opposition to planning may have been and also makes quite clear how little had been done by the National Planning Council. Actually the planning group remained in the President's office as the Directorate of Planning. However, it had weak leadership and no authority over ministries. While steps had been taken to increase individual ministries' planning capacity, by 1960 Tunisia had not advanced much further than Morocco toward creating an effective central planning agency. The full measure of the resistance will be clearer when the reaction to the ten-year plan for 1962–71 is described below, but some revelations can be found in the 1960 report of the Tunisian Federation of Industry and Commerce (*L'Union Tunisienne de l'Industrie et du Commerce*).

The businessmen approved Bourguiba's *lutte contre le sous-développement*, but they insisted that cooperation within this " 'framework' must be understood and clearly thought out." They stressed their need to be regularly informed prior to presidential and governmental intervention. They implicitly rejected the workers' intentions and spoke of the need to have an "empirically defined doctrine" and "realistic policy dictated by a natural evolution." [28] Recognizing that planning had been successfully performed in both capitalist and socialist countries, the report objected to doctrinaire approaches. Among the specific suggestions were proposals for increased use of public funds to supplement private capital. The planning agency was accepted, but it was made very clear that the businessmen expected to be represented on the key subcommissions. The business group was much less outspoken than the workers, and the report suggests that careful preliminary groundwork had been done to obtain a qualified measure of endorsement. To some extent the more conservative interests appear to have only been adjusting to realities, because the President announced early in 1961 that a full-scale planning organization would be created under the progressive Ben Salah, the *bête noire* of Tunisian conservatives.

Without minimizing the increasing economic pressures on Tunisia and its increasing disillusionment with France, it is important to note the strength of Bourguiba's position before he was prepared to make the planning decision in early 1961. A little more than a year before, he emerged virtually unchallenged in national elections. The party had been reorganized as he wished, using provincial and regional officers selected by the Neo-Destour's central headquarters. The problem had been raised, at least, with the party's most important auxiliary national organizations. The President had put off the final decision for three years, but he had used those years to make the public realize the importance of the "economic battle" and to ensure the support of the major organizations. The delay was just as great as in Morocco, but the monarchy did not succeed either in mobilizing popular opinion or in acquiring organized support.

Ben Salah came very close to receiving the powers of a second vice president as outlined in the UGTT proposal of 1956. A new "superministry" was created, headed by a secretary of state for planning and finance. Although reminiscent of the Moroccan "super-ministry," the Tunisian organization differed in that it was given effective power. Later in the year its powers were made greater when portions of the Industry and Commerce Ministry were assigned to it, and the old ministry dissolved. Ben Salah was permitted to draw upon the other ministries for key planning officials, many of whom had been his intellectual colleagues for years. An imaginative and devoted team was formed, and the full authority of the President was behind their work. Although evading emphatic references to socialism, Ben Salah made it clear that the plan was to embrace all sectors of the economy and would draw on earlier planning drafts.[29]

Drafting was done in five divisions: agriculture, industry, finance, infrastructure, and professional and technical skills (cadre). The Tunisians did not need to rely on United Nations or other technical assistance personnel, who produced most of the key documents in the Moroccan planning agency. There were none of the personnel problems that plagued the Moroccan Division of Economic Coordination and Planning, which was driven to training its own technicians at one point. Perhaps most important, Ben Salah did not need to worry about official support from either his party or his superior. His confidence was repeatedly bolstered by the President, and he was relieved of the additional political distractions imposed on Bouabid by his work for the National Union. There were still many skeptics and outright opponents both to Ben Salah and to planning in general, but the single-party regime gave the new minister the organizational and political support to produce a reputable plan.

The initial responses of Morocco and Tunisia to planning indicate how varied may be the adaptation of political regimes to planning requirements. In addition, these two experiences suggest that the kind of regime may to some degree determine how well new forms of influence and power created by national reconstruction may be related to the political process. It must be recognized that the fragmentation of political forces in Morocco over planning was only one instance of how politics there thwarted major institutional reforms, causing them rapidly to lose momentum and eventually to be forgotten. If planning is broadly conceived, the changes it seeks to introduce in an explicit and orderly fashion are not greatly different from the much less organized efforts of new parties and groups to place new demands on the political system. The inability of the monarchy to reconcile the relatively well-defined interests and issues of political parties indicates that the much more diffuse situation of relating a wide variety of new behavior among the citizens might be an even greater strain. In this sense the repercussions of planning are only a more easily identified aspect of the entire process of social change in a developing country.

The fact that the Tunisian political system found the challenge of planning equally threatening at an early stage is important, because it underscores the unavoidable political impact that planning activity entails. Though much more accustomed to accommodating new issues and problems than the monarchy, Tunisian leaders were apprehensive, too. Moreover, the decision to pursue planning vigorously brought about significant changes in leadership, in party organization, and eventually in the fundamental values of the political system. Bourguiba continued to extol the virtues of the struggle for independence, but he also introduced new values to support and interrelate new kinds of behavior. To a remarkable degree, the regime acknowledged that the ultimate purpose of planning was to create a new kind of citizen, a problem to be explored later in this study.

III

Participation and the Planning Effort

Equating planning with the entire problem of development may introduce complications for the economist and others with specific transformations indicating change and growth within their discipline, but the more comprehensive notion of planning has the advantage of focusing our attention on the experience of the nation that reflects how new behavior may indeed be reconciled in a new society. Morocco, for example, has undergone a variety of experiments to bring the impoverished citizen into closer contact with government and to enable him to improve his lot with official support. None of these programs would in themselves constitute a major planning activity in the economic sense, but each confronted the political system with an essential aspect of more ambitious planning. The minor efforts represented cautious efforts to diffuse authority in Moroccan society and tentatively created new centers of power outside the official lines of government. In none of these experiments has the Moroccan government followed through effectively, and in most cases the excessive hopes stimulated by the very persuasive traditional endorsement available to the monarch have been shattered, probably to become new obstacles for any future reforms along the same lines as past experiments.

The active participation phase of Tunisian planning represents a very different kind of problem from the fragmented political relations in Morocco. Having committed itself to energetic national reconstruction, the Neo-Destour entered a new phase in the creation of a participant society. As noted in the following section of the essay, the party experienced opposition and severe criticism, but it was the differentiation of the system around concrete, specific issues. The workability of the regime itself was not called into question, and it might be argued that Bourguiba's enthusiasm for development in fact kept nascent opposition parties and groups from becoming powerful. The essential point, however, is that active planning thrust the regime into an entirely new political framework. Not only was the legitimacy of the system reinforced, but the level of discourse and formulation of political differences changed. Questions of loyalty to the regime and the purity of nationalist values were replaced with questions of how values could be articulated into subordinate goals meaningful to the individual and how each specific advance in national reconstruction produced new goals and a new range of problems. Though still far from accomplishing all that has been outlined in the *Perspective Décennale,* the Tunisian regime has acquired many qualities associated with self-sustained development.

MOROCCO: RELUCTANCE AND INDECISION

After the Moroccan local elections of May 1960, Mohammed V became president of his own cabinet. The elections served to underscore party differences and define party strength, but without institutional channels for the orderly expression of party interests even the superficial form of cabinet government applied in Morocco was paralyzed. The young Prince became president of the cabinet and when his father died in early 1961 he became King Hassan II. The new King was no more willing than his father to make substantial delegations of power, and he tended to impose his personal wishes more arbitrarily than his father. Under the circumstances the monarchy has clashed more severely with the UMT and the National Union, while the other parties have tended to rely more heavily on the Palace for prestige and support. What the Moroccan government has gained in decisiveness has probably been paid for in increasingly arbitrary rule.

The new monarch lost nearly all the experienced officials of the Ministry of the National Economy, including Bouabid. He did nothing to bolster the Directorate of Economic Coordination and Planning, which has remained understaffed and powerless. The Minister of the National Economy, Douiri, was able and devoted but frequently found himself undercut or ignored by the Palace. Since the main lines of industrial and commercial development had been set down by the previous minister, he could do relatively little to alter plans and agreements already made with foreign and domestic investors. Some new planning documents were produced. A foreign econometrician calculated input-output matrices for 1958, 1960, and 1965, although it remains to be seen if they can be usefully applied in the absence of technical skills.[1] An industrial census which the French had begun in 1955, was completed in 1961 and provided material for an enlarged version of the industrial sector of the five-year plan.[2] The population census of 1956 was brought up to date in 1960, and showed that the Moroccans, like the Tunisians, had very seriously underestimated demographic growth for the coming decade.

But the effectiveness of planning activity of the developing country is not determined solely by documentation and statistics, which can be gathered in large quantity without the slightest intention of engaging in comprehensive planning and without political agreement of the most elemetary kind. Planning without popular approval and political consensus on the goals and methods of development is quite futile. There is little in Moroccan political life to suggest that planning will be taken seriously and much that indicates increasingly acrimonious controversy between official and opposition views. The King has tended to surround himself with relatively submissive ministers, while making symbolic concessions to the few petitions the Istiqlal and the other minor cooperative parties submit.

The Istiqlal has not managed to escape the dilemma of being caught between its loyality to the Alaouite dynasty and its need to develop its own popular support. With the schism in the nationalist movement the elder leaders came back into operational positions in the party, and traditional concerns tended to drown out such contemporary issues as planning. Allal Al-Fassi has been much more concerned with irredentist agitation than economic growth, while many of the other old-guard leaders are preoccupied with business affairs and more glamorous activities abroad. In the party Congress of January 1960 planning was not even mentioned.[3] Some publicity is given to planning when the Superior Planning Council meets, but it only reveals the party's secondary role. Shortly before the August

1960 meeting Douiri came out in the party newspaper favoring special programs to integrate the modern and traditional sectors of the economy and also to decentralize control.[4] Neither of these proposals received attention in the meeting or subsequently in ministerial actions.

The Istiqlal's lack of interest in planned development contrasts with the National Union's devotion to planning as the panacea for all national ills. The opposition group has the informed leadership of both Bouabid and Ibrahim, who laid the groundwork for the rudimentary developmental effort now being continued. They must also work with the UMT, whose denunciation of the present government certainly verges on libel and does much to discredit their position. Excluded from the seat of power, the National Union and the UMT have concentrated their efforts in Casablanca, where they control the municipal council. Steps have been taken to organize municipally owned corporations for public transport and electricity distribution. However, the progressives' experience in municipal enterprise has not served to tone down their vehemence in national affairs.

As in the rest of the non-Western world, the left has the advantage of being able to adopt a ready-made doctrine along with carefully selected examples of its benefits from the Communist world. However, the fruits of socialism are examined more critically as the new nation gains experience. Thus, Bouabid rejects capitalist solutions as unsuitable because of time limitations and the uneven development that may result.[5] He opposes the use of tradition to justify piecemeal, disorganized development, but he admits that socialism must be adapted to Moroccan needs. He describes it as a "general orientation whose methods of application vary according to local conditions and the traditions observed in the country of application." The fear of the National Union is that Morocco's development effort will become an interlocking structure of favored businessmen, wealthy landowners, and the Palace. In much less xenophobic form than his labor supporters, Bouabid also rejects capital that would tend to entrench political groups or to sacrifice Morocco's control of its own development.

The suspicions of the party favoring a social revolution are difficult to confirm in the light of Moroccan events since 1961. It is clear that opportunities and precious time have been lost, but the King has done less to erect new obstacles for equalitarian reform and planning than simply to disconnect developmental efforts. This in itself is costly of both human and material resources, but it is by no means as unilaterally advantageous politically to conservative interests as the radical group presume in their propaganda. Traditional political systems are often more easily manipulated by the supreme figures in the system, but their stability also provides time for social tensions to grow and for popular estimates to be made. The fact that traditional systems respond slowly to new demands does not mean that inadequacy goes unnoticed. Many favors may be done through the Palace, but similar favors are also granted to friends of the progressives through the municipal government of Casablanca.[6] The critical decision in Moroccan development and planning activity is when to make concessions to the gradual process of political education and experience the monarchy has made possible.

Although participation may not be a condition of successful planning and development, the Moroccan case illustrates the effects of a deteriorating political situation. The government had known since early 1961 that it would have difficulty fulfilling the modest, though ill-defined, proposals of the five-year plan.[7] However, two years elapsed before a decision was made, during which inflationary pressures undermined the few developmental projects in advanced stages. Early in 1963 the Istiqlal left the government coalition, and Douiri gave the King's reluctance to adhere to a long-range plan as one of the reasons behind the party's break from its traditional support of the monarchy. In mid-1963 the Palace announced that the five-year plan was terminated and that a three-year proposal would be drafted with the assistance of French technicians.[8]

The Palace's abandoning of a plan that had never been put into effect was not very surprising, but other tendencies within the political system revealed a new orientation toward development as a whole. Under King Hassan II power was further concentrated in the Palace,[9] and development projects were closely scrutinized by an "economic czar," Laghzaoui, whose activities are directly coordinated with high officials. Although new proposals to improve agriculture and to regionalize development were discussed, the emphasis came to be on industrial projects arranged individually through high-level contacts in the Moroccan government. Political forces have been largely excluded from the planning process, and only symbolic measures remain to arouse popular support and understanding of the development effort.

There are many ways of evaluating the Moroccan government's response to the planning needs created by the social and political changes introduced by independence. Among such indicators are regional planning, local cooperatives, and other community-run enterprise, and the use of "labor capital" or varieties of public works projects. All three devices require planning and coordination for maximum effectiveness. They also require leaders who have some fairly well-defined ideas about the future political life of their country and how the individual citizen will relate to government as he acquires new skills and more influence in a modernizing society. A government does not have to be of any particular doctrinal or institutional type to make the concessions appropriate to the development of a more intricate, more diversified social system. Indeed, if one of the critical steps in economic as well as political development is how the transition is made from a centrally directed process of change to a more diffuse, self-regulatory form of growth, the single-party system may create more hazards to cumulative development than the monarchy.

The five-year plan contains an enthusiastic endorsement of regional planning.[10] Acknowledging regional disparities and the aggravating effect of the rural exodus, the plan recognizes the need to direct improvements to the provincial and local level. However, there are only vague suggestions for regional councils, which had been originally suggested in the law establishing the Superior Planning Council in 1957. The plan also notes that such groups would have to submit to the Ministry of National Economy and Finance both the financial and technical aspects of regional projects. The requisite would be more reasonable in a less cumbersome administration but would surely paralyze provincial efforts in Morocco. Although some provinces have set up advisory groups to discuss the provincial budget, there has been no provincial or regional organization. The new National Office of Irrigation and its counterpart for dry-farming areas, the National Office of Rural Modernization, hold promise of stimulating regional organizations but are still operated from Rabat. They have been known to undertake projects that are unknown to provincial governors.

Regional planning has been labeled "essential" by Douiri [11] as well as by his predecessor, Bouabid. Neither was ever given the necessary authority to create regional planning groups, and there is considerable evidence of intentional obstruction by other ministries that feel their interests would be slighted. Further, the governors and provincial officials have remained so tightly under the control of the Minister of the Interior and so preoccupied with policing tasks that they have little time or inclination to take on more onerous duties. Although there were reports that ministers were being sent out to solicit provincial programs in late 1962,[12] it is doubtful if so improvised a method will produce meaningful results.

The experience of the rural communes has been very similar. The law organizing the eight hundred local councils gave them the right to form *syndicats* or unions for developmental purposes.[13] In many provinces local problems can be handled only by coordinating the effort of several communes, and frequently funds must be pooled. While the five-year plan points with pride to the communal elections, which were to "produce representatives of the local population and to facilitate their active participation in developmental actions," [14] very little has been done to remove the communes from the close supervision of the Ministry of the Interior. Both the National Union and the Istiqlal have demanded increased budgetary and financial powers for the communes, no doubt to build local party strength as much as to increase developmental activity. Although some municipal councils under National Union control engaged in enterprises already in operation, the government has done little to stimulate or to support more widespread, diffuse interest in planning.

A third possibility for increased local developmental activity to support central planning has been the *Promotion Nationale,* a program of public relief supported with American wheat. Received with great fanfare in mid-1961, the plan was heralded as the opening of a new era of voluntary local participation in national reconstruction.[15] Although the Moroccans have received large quantities of wheat and have put several hundred thousands of underemployed *fellahiin* to work, the program has not been fully exploited. Because of ministerial jealousies and royal reluctance, the central office was denied both the staff and the authority needed to ensure the formulation of worthwhile projects, and the provincial administration found its proposals hopelessly enmeshed in the bureaucracy of the captial. The original director of the program resigned when it became clear that the King had no intention of making the program the vehicle for a rural reawaking and meaningful agrarian reform.[16] While the *Promotion Nationale* will undoubtly continue to make some worthwhile contributions to Moroccan development, it has become bogged down in the debilitating combination of hesitancy and fancifulness that characterizes so much Moroccan political life.

These examples are more indicative of the Moroccan government's approach to the challenge of planning than of the economic impact the plan itself may make. In revealing the government's intentions they are probably more valuable than a well-designed plan that may never be put into operation. Both the Tunisians and the Moroccans have displayed extreme caution in undertaking planning activity that might suggest major reorientation of the political system. However, procrastination and disillusionment have certainly been more frequent in Morocco, where promising ideas are prematurely and uncritically seized for propaganda effect and then forgotten. Tunisia has managed to reorganize her economic institutions to fill planning needs. The administration has been reformed, too, and sufficient Tunisian talent has been attracted to dispense with nearly all foreign contract personnel. In comparison, Moroccan planning activity has been sporadic and erratic. Some institutions were organized, while others were neglected. Nearly all Moroccan proposals for reform and development projects have been inordinately delayed and have suffered the ravages of a jealous bureaucracy.

While this essay is not primarily concerned with predicting Morocco's future, it is obvious that a new nation's capacity to plan and to adapt will be essential in preserving the existing political institutions. In this regard it is difficult to make highly optimistic estimates of Morocco. The monarchy enjoys privileges and considerable popular appeal that might be used to rally popular support and interest as Moroccan plans develop. The King could certainly undertake fundamental administrative reforms as easily as Bourguiba. Morocco is a nation of great potential, but the capricious political system may prevent adaption to the needs of planning and, indirectly, to the pressures of an expanding population and growing political awareness.

TUNISIA: ANTICIPATION AND REFORM

The Tunisian Secretariat for Planning and Finance followed a carefully drawn schedule in preparing the *perspective* or forecast on which Tunisian planning was to be based. The team that Ben Salah assembled in the Planning Commission had almost six months to prepare the first planning document, which was completed in September 1961. This permitted two months of discussion of the broad concepts of the *perspective,* which were to be followed up with a phased plan for the ten years beginning in 1962. The plan for 1962–64 was prepared late in 1961 and presented in early 1962. As it turned out, this was hardly enough time. The planning team did a good job, but the party and the country were not nearly as well prepared as the uniformity of the single-party system might imply. The difficulties the Tunisian officials had despite the political preparation provided by the Neo-Destour suggest how far Morocco has yet to go.

When Ben Salah was installed, the President began alerting high officials to the need to prepare the party's supporters and the people generally. In January 1961 the Economic and Social Council, an organ created by the constitution and never assembled, was organized.[17] The council was particularly well suited to its primarily political task, because it brought together all the most influential Tunisians for the specific purpose of discussing economic proposals of all kinds. In the fall the party also enlisted its auxiliary organizations, which were a more confidential means of feeling out the party than the public meetings of the council. Through the extraordinary organization of the Neo-Destour study, commissions of party representatives were created at the level of electoral districts, and the leaders of the local National Front list [18] met with the municipal councils, local influentials of a kinds, and government officials to introduce the plan. At the same time the *Perspective Décennale* was distributed to the Tunis headquarters of the UGTT and the other national organizations. Such a two-pronged attack, would, of course, be nearly impossible in Morocco. Essentially the same procedure was followed with the *Plan Triennal* in early 1962.

From the beginning Ben Salah had the support of the President. Bourguiba made it clear in his famous weekly speeches that the plan would be submitted to popular judgment and would not follow any doctrine except the well-worn goals of "Bourguibism," a mixture of political dexterity and compromise. Nevertheless, the President's speeches throughout 1961 explained more precisely the advantages of collective action in other spheres than agriculture. With characteristic skill he played on the beneficial results of nationalizing the *habous* land, while noting precedents for cooperative effort in Islam.[19] Gradually the new national goal took shape in his speeches and emerged as "Neo-Destourian Socialism." His presentation is a precise, reasoned case for planning in Tunisia, while it acknowledges the hardships and conflicts that economic control and supervision will entail.

First, the need for discipline was stressed. In the custom of the single-party state, once decisions are taken for the welfare of the country no lapse of effort or carelessness is tolerated. This stricture applies to "traditionalist" opposition as well as to opportunists. Second, the President pictured the change as one affecting the dignity and well-being of every Tunisian, acknowledging that many individuals had not yet been indoctrinated with the necessary motives and aspirations. With great candor he called for "a true psychological revolution . . . to assure the success of the plan" and a purposeful campaign "similar to that which in the past allowed me to obtain the support of an elite and a considerable section of the population to whom I gave new conceptions and another scale of values." Seldom has the problem been described so explicitly for public consumption. Third, the President condemmed hoarding savings and gold, while admitting that the plan would entail restrictions of individual liberty. Lastly, Bourguiba again gave his public endorsement of Ben Salah and condemmed those who charged the chief planner with too socialist ideals. The President acknowledged the historic importance of socialism but gave planning and its benefits much broader significance by appealing to national pride and individidual self-respect. Rejecting communism, he noted in closing that "humanity's fate lies in the survival of the motives for collaboration among men." [20] Few national leaders have given such unequivocal, cogent explanations for planning.

Despite the strong support given by the President, there was increasing resistance during the autumn of 1961. Speaking to party militants, the director of the Neo-Destour Political Bureau reassured the party that "the plan will be the work of neither a person nor a group of experts, but that of the party in its conception as well as its execution." [21] Shortly afterward Ben Salah received the ultimate expression of confidence by being restored to the Political Bureau. Nevertheless, newspaper reports acknowledged that the technical commissions of the Superior Committee of the Plan, the political advisory group to the Planning Commission, had expressed reservations on the perspective use of production cooperatives and tendency to restrain private initiative.[22] In a speech at Bizerte Ben Salah publicly challenged the critics of the plan and presented it as part of the national effort to eliminate colonial influence.[23] Such public confessions of resistance are extremely rare in Tunisian politics and indicate an unusual degree of resistance. Further, the fact that officials used public devices to counteract their critics suggests that the Political Bureau hoped to use popular pressure against opposition outside the party structure. The opposition was especially strong from commercial interests, who suspected that Ben Salah's known antipathy for the merchants, new import and price controls, and suggestions for consumer cooperatives foretold their end.[24]

The merchants are formidable opposition, and they had given Bourguiba's policy of "gradualism" strong support because it tended to serve their interests as well as Tunisia's. It took considerable courage to withstand their wrath, but the party organization held fast. From October 1961 until early spring the leading members of the party made weekly forays into the countryside. The intensive program of indoctrination and persuasion was an impressive display of how the single-party system can attack a difficult problem at all levels and with endless resources. In the manner of all the single-party schemes, the legislature was called upon to express and confirm unanimity. The Economic and Social Council, an arm of the National Assembly which had never met previously, convened in February 1962.[25] This meeting was followed by a session of the Neo-Destour's National Council, another group that had seldom been called upon and included many local notables. Among them there were undoubtedly numerous businessmen and merchants.

The National Council meeting was very likely the critical hurdle for the party. It was reported at the time that "it is not secret that in the party—and not only at the base—certain reserves, some reticence were sometimes manifested regarding the Plan." [26] The council's approval would mean that any subsequent opposition would encounter severe repression for "obstructing the nation." The party performed in its most persuasive manner for the meeting. Long, carefully prepared speeches were given by Ben Salah, the President, and Bahi Ladgham, his most trusted lieutenant, Secretary General of the party, and the Vice President. Bourguiba again gave an impassioned plea for "Neo-Destourian socialism," a doctrine that he called midway between anarchy and excessive state interference. Ladgham returned to the theme that the plan was only a new phase in the party's continuing struggle to liberate Tunisia and did not represent a new orientation. Repeating a message he had often used in the regional and local meetings of the past six months, Ben Salah said that the plan was not directed against any class and was not designed "to annihilate" the merchants.

From the party's National Council, the plan returned to government channels and was studied by the five subcommissions of the National Assembly, representing social affairs, industry and commerce, training of professional and technical cadre, agriculture, and finance. The three-year plan was finally presented to the National Assembly. The ceaseless efforts to reduce the opposition before formal institutions considered the controversy yielded the usual unanimity of the Tunisian legislature. While one might express some reservations over the techiques of the party (the President himself had assured the National Council that the plan would not be imposed by force, propaganda, or insult but by Tunisia's success alone), the new country's ability to focus coordinated, skilled talent on a major problem distinguishes it from most of the developing countries.

Although this volume is not intended to evaluate the soundness of the planning documents produced by either Morocco or Tunisia, the Tunisian product is without question a much more precise, coherent, and unequivocal proposal. Of course, officials in both countries are aware of the shortcomings of their planning agencies and neither would want the available documents considered final or complete plans. But this reservation applies to most documentation emanating from the non-Western world and also reflects the leaders' reluctance to be tied down and judged on specific points. The planning documents of both countries are nevertheless meaningful indicators of the government's effectiveness and decisiveness. The plans are, after all, presumably the best the leaders can prepare and represent what they approve of insofar as the future development of the nation can be mapped out.

The Tunisian perspective has been published in two editions, the second incorporating some changes suggested by American and international aid experts. The first edition of the ten-year forecast followed the UGTT proposal of 1956 more closely than the second, but both are remarkable documents. While the Moroccan plan goes little further than compiling estimates of investment needs by sectors and listing some of the major projects involved, the Tunisian plan departs conceptually from the country's French framework and establishes the goal of redistributing additional income more equitably. It clearly and convincingly presents the disequilibrium of past development in terms of regional, sectoral, and financial disparities. It proceeds from demographic estimates and manpower requirements for the desired growth, with the needs of each income group being interpolated from a development model.

There was no hedging on issues of administrative or financial reform, and particular attention was paid to developing human resources. Both these aspects of the Moroccan plan are especially weak. The problem of land reform is treated as a whole and proposals for rural cooperatives are put forward. The Moroccan plan had few specific proposals for agriculture except for the existing plowing program and rural machine centers. Fundamental problems are evaded, or possibly further confused, by giving primary responsibility for agricultural improvement to semiautonomous agencies. Morocco still depends heavily on French concepts and French methods, while opening the way for costly duplication of effort and more fruitless conflict within the government.

Though there has been localized resistance to some measures adopted under the plan from merchants, small farmers, and transport owners, the essential difference from Morocco is clear. The Tunisian government is dealing with development problems at the level of the participant himself. Historical advantages alone do not satisfactorily explain the Tunisian success in diffusing and decentralizing development activities. The attempt on Bourguiba's life in late December 1962 led him to reassess his position, and it is interesting to note that the President publicly declined to change his view that political forces are fundamental in the process of economic and social change.[27] Despite possible reservations about the one-party system, the fact remains that Tunisia has produced a system in which political relationships receive careful consideration. As a result, the Tunisian government has accrued distinct material advantages while opening the way for increasingly broad participation in the developmental process.[28]

The relative success of the Tunisian planning effort does not mean that high officials were entirely agreed but only that they were sufficiently united behind the Neo-Destour and their President to contribute to their country's reconstruction.[29] There were rumors in Tunis that banking circles, which would include the influential Nouira of the Central Bank, had doubts over the possible inflationary effects of the plan. The Ministry of Education already had a plan, and reportedly resisted early requests to integrate their plan with the human-resources section of the ten-year plan. Very powerful ministries, such as Public Works, and the Interior, also viewed the growing strength of Ben Salah's organization with some skepticism. One of the major unanswered questions in early 1962, as the secretary of planning and finance prepared to take the first measures to implement the plan, was how coordination would be effected between the ministry and the governors, who have been practically the exclusive agents of the President and possess powers comparable to those of a minister. The ministry hoped to place a *délégué,* comparable to the party representative, under each governor to supervise implementation and report progress. If this were done, the regional officials would lose power to the benefit of the Ben Salah organization. Many older officials still considered him a young upstart and a political threat and confidentially expressed doubts about the ten-year plan.

But the Tunisian impediments to planning are elementary compared to the decisions that remain to be made before Morocco will attain a comparable stage in her planning. The explanation of Tunisian progress requires more than acknowledging her poverty, for there are many equally poor and even poorer nations that have failed to respond to internal economic pressures. Tunisia has had centuries of experience with territorial and governmental organizations of many kinds, and the tradition has been continued under the Neo-Destour. Under three generations of colonial occupation Tunisians saw much of the European world, while Morocco was still largely cut off by a disintegrating monarchical government that seldom controlled the entire country. Moroccan development was further handicapped by the division of the country between Spanish and French zones—a division that still plagues economic integration—and also between Berber- and Arab-speaking areas. None of these factors alone is a satisfactory explanation of the Moroccan and Tunisian planning efforts. The answer must be sought in a combination of historical, organizational, and political circumstances.

However, it would be a mistake to identify the Tunisian reaction as politically progressive and necessarily constructive for her long-term development and the Moroccan experience as one condemning the country to an endless series of futile, confused endeavors. Planning, like many of the other major internal questions arising after independence, demands certain attitudinal adjustments by large numbers of persons. The problems of attitudinal change in the developing countries are only dimly understood, but it is in the adjustment of existing attitudes toward government and the nation's future that the imponderables of history, organization, and politics are combined.[30]

Despite the opposition in some quarters, the single-party system has shown itself well suited to mobilizing popular opinion and influential groups on behalf of planning. A new country that still relies on the dramatic mass appeals of religion, irredentism, or nationalism will naturally find the dully repetitive and endlessly detailed procedures of planning and related developmental activity politically unattractive. Although Bourguiba often presents the plan and related reforms in terms of national dignity and the struggle against colonialist influence, he is also beginning to familiarize his people with a more complex psychological world. The specialization and diversity of the modern society demands unusual individual flexibility. It can be asked, however, how well the highly centralized system will adapt to the effects of economic development and to the occasional failure that may embarrass leaders. In time citizens and groups begin to acquire the critical skills and individual interests of a more articulate, less oppressed people. The single party may operate with effectiveness at Tunisia's present stage of development, but it may also be contributing to the social transformation that will make its hegemony more difficult to sustain.

The Moroccan case is more difficult to forecast, because the diversity of Morocco's peoples and its developmental possibilities offer more alternatives. The combination of monarchy and parties may cause some distress to those who think in terms of their own political careers or who have fixed ideas about economic development. But it must be acknowledged that Morocco could derive benefits from a regime that permits less advanced regions to acquire the social awareness and political identification to defend their interests. While the authoritarian overtones of Tunisian political techniques may form psychological rigidities that may eventually hurt the country, the appeal of the Alaouite *imam* (spiritual leader or monarch) in Morocco can reach the far corners of a divided land and give the less advanced a chance to catch up. The country may pay something in time and wealth in order to retain greater possibilities of political stability and moderation. Whether or not opportunities for balanced political development are used depends, of course, on King Hassan II, whose methods have sometimes left even his supporters without clear direction or encouragement.

Planning will certainly remain a crucial focus for political as well as economic development in Morocco, Tunisia, and the rest of the developing countries. It incorporates many key features of the modern world: official accountability, political responsibility, doctrinal clarification, and individual adaptability. These qualities were not needed in the struggle for independence, but they will be of crucial importance in the future of Africa and Asia.

IV

An Approach through the
Social Sciences

This discussion of planning in North Africa has placed great stress on the role of the participant, how it is affected by new behavior inherent in the development process, and how such new behavior relates to the values of the two different political systems of Morocco and Tunisia. The social sciences are only now beginning to formulate reliable generalizations about the relation of beliefs, perceptions, and behavior,[1] but the combination of values and behavior is clearly a central problem of every developmental effort. Indeed, the student interested in some of the more sweeping questions in social science might well find that the developing country offers problems of a magnitude such that some of the more elusive aspects of variations in these two elements of human behavior are more easily isolated and observed.

The following paradigm is intended only to underscore the nature of the problem of relating changing values to changing behavior in the context of development and planning. As will be noted, there are some aspects of the paradigm that have been more extensively investigated in research in more highly developed countries. It should also be noted that specifying a high or low degree of attitudinal change in itself raises a host of problems that the psychologist has yet to solve. As the paradigm suggests, some of these problems might be overcome if the sharp distinction between environment and personality could be eliminated. There has, in fact, been a major effort within psychology to do this in the past decade,[2] though the suggestions stemming from the approach have yet to be applied to studies of developing nations.

SOCIAL CHANGE

		HI	LO
Attitudinal	HI	Institutionalized Change	Symbolic Change
Change	LO	Ritual Change	Minimal Change

Perhaps the most important qualification to be made immediately is that attitudinal change cannot be measured in a linear form like many kinds of social change. Thus, more persons employed in factories, attending schools, and saving money may be taken as evidence of social change. However, as many experiments in developing countries have shown, the simple occurrence of new behavior does not mean that the society has necessarily established a permanent change. Perhaps the most plentiful illustrations are from the field of technical assistance, once thought to be the touchstone of development. Endless examples could be found of the peasant who has meticulously planted as directed, observed the more bountiful harvest, and then abandoned the practice once supervision ceased. In effect, the change was a ritual performance. The gratifying evidence of new behavior represented no change in the peasant's view toward his agrarian pursuits, their relation to his family, his village, or his country.

Hence, a high degree of attitudinal change would not be properly considered as increased intensity in his conviction about straight-line planting, and he may, in fact, feel very intensely that it is the correct behavior while he is doing it. To achieve a high degree of attitudinal change he must very likely undergo a reorganization of many other values, acquire a good deal of cognitive skill in other areas, and develop a psychological flexibility perhaps best specified in Daniel Lerner's conception of "empathy." [3] Thus, institutionalized change is more than new behavior, and probably even more than normatively oriented behavior in the sociologist's sense. A value must be attached to the new behavior, but the value may also need to be related to other values, some of them possibly traditional and others new. The source of the values enabling the participant to give coherence to new behavior is not as important as their structure and their use.

The difficult problem of meaningful attitudinal change may be clarified to some extent by considering the opposed case of significant change in attitude unaccompanied by new behavior. This sequence of introducing change is obviously more difficult to observe but has been considered in personality studies where the individual's refusal to change behavior in the light of compelling evidence has brought about attitudinal restructuring.[4] Thus, the individual rearranges the significance and relation of his perceptions to protect a closely held value. The result is that he cannot benefit from what he has been exposed to at a later time or use new information of this type in interpreting his basic values. Very simply, he stops learning in order to forestall changing behavior. Thus, attitudes are restructured unlike the case of ritual change, but they are restructured in a way that inhibits new behavior and prevents learning from experience.

The evidence has yet to be gathered from the developing countries to bear out the alternatives indicated in the paradigm. However, the planning experience of Morocco and Tunisia suggests two of the alternatives. The Moroccan has gone through many motions similar to those found in the development process in Tunisia, but in most cases the new behavior was introduced through the compelling force of the religion and the monarchy. The peasant went through such rituals as voting and discussing local development through public works without having this behavior reinforced to the extent that his attitudes were fundamentally restructured. Such a change is conceivable on a societal level, as James N. Mosel has suggested for Thailand.[5] However, the experience of other Moslem countries suggests that the same limitations probably do not apply in North Africa.

Tunisia, it is suggested, has been approaching a state of affairs represented by institutionalized change. To accomplish this it has been necessary for the party to place much less emphasis on earlier nationalist principles and to extol development and socialism. Almost imperceptibly discourse about planning and development in Tunisia has shifted from the remote and abstract level of national virtue, its symbol and purity, to the arguments for and against devaluation, various forms of rural cooperatives, and the advantages of diversifying its foreign markets. The terminal value, national devotion, has not changed nearly so much as the subordinate values have been multiplied, evaluated, and translated into action. The extent to which this transformation of national political life has been understood and accepted by the average Tunisian could only be determined by careful surveys, but if the Tunisian planning effort continues to be widely diffused in the population and begins to produce sustained performances on the part of many citizens, there will be some grounds for predicting that substantial attitudinal change is taking place. In fact, it becomes increasingly critical that the Tunisian government know that the newly elicited behavior is not ritual as the country becomes more and more committed to development and the political system dependent on its results.

Few developing countries have yet advanced far enough into the complexities of national reconstruction to attempt the kind of assessment of planning effectiveness suggested by the paradigm. However, it is crucial to future stages of development that the new country have some evidence that new behavior and values are indeed finding some links in the minds of the impoverished citizen. Without such links change may be only temporary ritualized performance, or efforts may produce only a convenient psychological adjustment to avoid changing behavior.

Notes to Chapters

I. WHERE PLANNING BEGINS

1. For an analysis of the Istiqlal schism and additional background on Morocco see the author's *Political Change in Morocco* (Princeton: Princeton University Press, 1961). The most nearly complete study of Tunisia in English is Charles Micaud, Clement Moore, and Leon Carl Brown, *The Politics of Modernization: Tunisia* (New York: Praeger, 1964).

2. Although there have been important inquiries using Freudian principles, there has been relatively little inquiry suitable for higher generalization and directed toward the problems of conceptual and attitudinal change. One such study is Lucian W. Pye's *Politics, Personality and Nation Building* (New Haven: Yale University Press, 1962).

3. See Rupert Emerson, *From Empire to Nation* (Cambridge: Harvard University Press, 1960).

II. POLITICAL FORCES IN THE COMMITMENT TO PLANNING

1. For more detail on planning in the Protectorate, see the careful study of Albert Waterston, *Planning in Morocco* (Baltimore: The Johns Hopkins Press, 1962). This is part of a series of planning studies sponsored by the Economic Development Institute of the International Bank for Reconstruction and Development.

2. France, President of the Council, General Commisariat of the Plan, Deuxième Plan de Modernisation et d'Equipment, *Rapport Général de la Commission d'Etude et de Coordination des Plans de Modernisation et d'Equipment de l'Algérie, de la Tunisie et du Maroc* (Maroc, 1954), pp. 6, 17.

3. *Bulletin Officiel du Maroc,* no. 2333, July 12, 1957, "Dahir no. 1-57-183 (22 juin 1957) préscrivant l'établissement d'un plan de développement économique et social et instituant un conseil supérieur du plan," p. 861.

4. See the almost identical organizational charts given in Waterston, *Planning,* p. 17.

5. Morocco, Division of Economic Coordination and Planning, Min-

istry of the National Economy and Finance, *Plan Biennal d'Equipment, 1958–1959* (Rabat, 1958), p. 78.

6. See the author's "The New Irredentism: Morocco and Mauritania," *The Western Political Quarterly,* XV, no. 4 (December 1962), 641–51.

7. Reported in *La Vigie Marocaine,* November 23, 1958, p. 1, and *Le Monde,* November 27, 1958, p. 1.

8. *Al-Istiqlal,* May 18, 1958, p. 3.

9. The results of "Operation Plow" are controversial. See Mohammed Fadli, *Opération Labour* (Rabat: Centre d'Etude de Développement Economique et Social, Université de Rabat, 1961), and also Georges Oved, "Problèmes de Développement Economique au Maroc," *Tiers Monde* (Paris: Institut d'Etude du Développement Economique et Social, July–September 1961), pp. 355–98.

10. Morocco, Conseil Supérieur du Plan, *Exposé de M. Bouabid, Vice-Président du Conseil,* 23 Novembre 1959 (Rabat, 1959), Mimeo. Also reported in *L'Avante-garde,* November 29, 1959, p. 5.

11. More detailed results and analysis of the 1960 elections are contained in the author's "Elections in Morocco: Progress or Confusion," *Middle East Journal,* XV (Winter 1961), 1–15.

12. Morocco, Division of Economic Coordination and Planning, Ministry of the National Economy and Finance, *Compte Rendu des Délibérations du Conseil Supérieur du Plan* (Rabat, 1–5 Août 1960) p. 19, Mimeo.

13. Morocco, Division of Economic Coordination and Planning, Ministry of the National Economy and Planning, *Plan Quinquennal 1960–1964* (Rabat, 1960), p. 401.

14. Elie Fitoussi and Aristide Benazet, *L'Etat Tunisien et la Protectorate Française* (Paris: Libraire Arthur Rousseau, 1931), I, 235–37.

15. Charles F. Gallagher, "Two Tunisias: The Plan for the Development of the Center-South," *American Universities Field Staff Reports* (August 15, 1956), p. 7.

16. Neo-Destour, *Les Congrès du Neo-Destour* (Tunis, 1958), p. 79.

17. "Rapport Economique," *6ème Congrès National de l'UGTT,* September 20–23, 1956, pp. 7–8.

18. The split of the Tunisian trade unions has yet to be carefully studied. For some background see Clement Moore, "The Neo-Destour Party of Tunisia: A Structure for Democracy?" *World Politics,* XV (April 1962), 466; and also the author's "Transitional Politics in Morocco and Tunisia," *Princeton University Conference Series* (1959), pp. 14–35.

19. It is interesting to compare the kind of French advisors found in the two countries. The late King Mohammed V reportedly had confi-

dence in the Comte de Paris, while his son and he have called on the French constitutional experts, Duverger and La Baudière. Bourguiba's French friends have a decided intellectual quality (for example, Jean Rous and Gabriel Ardant, whose comment appears from time to time in *Afrique Action*). See the issues of November 21, 1960, pp. 8–9 and May 1, 1961, pp. 14–15.

20. The law appears in the *Journal Officiel Tunisien* and also in a brochure, *Le Conseil National du Plan* (Tunis: Secretary of State for Information, n.d.).

21. Tunisian party officials were quite outspoken in the fall of 1958 concerning the difficulty of working with the provincial committees. They seem to have represented a body of opinion not unlike that now found in the Istiqlal. Perhaps the most revealing commentary on the proposed reorganization is Bourguiba's speech to local party officials, *Les Congrès du Neo-Destour,* pp. 86–95.

22. The dilemma of economic growth vs. political development is by no means inevitable, but this is one of the clearest examples known to the author of where a clear choice had to be made. The old-guard Neo-Destourians quite clearly represented grass-roots opinion, which did not share much of the President's impatience to reform religious institutions or the economy. At the same time, they were valuable interlocutors between the government and the villages, an asset relatively few new countries have. Their subordination to centrally conceived plans sacrificed opportunities of less easily controlled, but possibly just as effective, development from the local level. This problem is receiving more attention in a comparative study the author is now preparing.

23. The Moroccan use of the wheat program was characteristically much more ambitious in conception and probably less effective in application. It will be discussed further below. While the Tunisians have distributed the food through *chantiers,* which could be more easily supervised, the Moroccans have tried to design projects using local suggestions but without really giving the localities any authority.

24. Tunis, Secretary of State for Education, *Ten Year Prospect of School Attendance* (Tunis, 1958); now followed up by an assessment, *Situation Scolaire: 3 premières années de l'application du plan décennal de scolarisation* (Tunis, 1961).

25. Bourguiba's speeches are widely distributed, and after his periodical regional tours they are printed in small books. For examples see Habib Bourguiba, *Electoral Campaign Speeches,* October 26–November 5, 1959 (Tunis: Secretary of State for Information, 1960); and also *Le Discours de Victoire* (Tunis: Secretary of State for Information, 1959), the President's speech to the Sousse Congress of March 1959. It is inter-

esting to note that the information services have begun publishing almost equal amounts in English and French since the Bizerte crisis.

26. Union Général des Travailleurs Tunisiens, Rapport d'Activité: *8ème Congrès National,* 1–3 Avril 1960 (Tunis, n.d.), pp. 10–11.

27. Union Général des Travailleurs Tunisiens, *Sur le Chemin du Développement* (Tunis, n.d.), p. 31.

28. Union Tunisienne de l'Industrie et du Commerce, *5ème Congrès National: Rapport Economique* (October 28–30, 1960), pp. 10–15.

29. *Afrique Action,* January 10, 1961, p. 11. This newspaper is the successor to the old *Action Tunisienne,* suspended in the fall of 1958 for criticizing presidential policy. In the spring of 1962 it was again involved in a dispute over the President's *pouvoir personnel* and has changed its name to *Jeune Afrique,* thereby totally removing a party slogan from its title.

III. PARTICIPATION AND THE PLANNING EFFORT

1. See Waterston, *Planning,* p. 33.

2. Division of Economic Coordination and Planning, Ministry of the National Economy and Finance, *Plan Quinquennal 1960–1964: Le Développement Industriel* (Rabat, n.d., [1962]).

3. *Al-Istiqlal,* January 16, 1960, Special Insert of Party Motions.

4. *Ibid.,* July 30, 1960, p. 4.

5. *Al-Machahid,* October 1961.

6. One of the more interesting results of the author's voting study of the 1960 elections, "Elections in Morocco," was that the National Union tended to sweep the ballots in all elections where they had strength. In Casablanca they won the elections for the Chamber of Commerce as well as the municipal council, though campaigning on what a Westerner would regard as a rather antibusiness platform. The Istiqlal managed to have the first Chamber of Commerce elections annulled and proceeded to lose a second time. It appears that the Istiqlal has allowed itself to be identified with the large merchants of Casablanca.

7. *La Situation Economique du Maroc en 1960* (Rabat: Division of Economic Coordination and the Plan, Ministry of National Economy, July 1961).

8. See *Al-Istiqlal,* June 30, 1963. After the departure of the Istiqlal, the King took measures to constitute a new planning council as provided in 1962 Constitution, arts. 76–99. The party objected strenuously to the exclusion of political representatives, *Al-Alam,* November 22, 1963.

9. There have been two distinct shifts, whose precise implications for planning are unclear. Until late 1963 the King worked through Ahmed

Guedira, whose earlier statements on planning indicated the Palace's distaste for the five-year plan and long-term programs in general. See *La Vie Economique,* February 15, 1963. In the late fall a new government was formed almost entirely of technicians and high civil servants devoted to the King, and Guedira was given a less important role. Morocco was still undergoing the agony of making the initial decision to plan in 1965. In the spring the King decided to take the post of prime minister, renewed efforts to formulate a "program" for development, and nationalized foreign trade in an effort to gain some control over Moroccan economic development.

10. *Plan Quinquennal,* pp. 351–76.

11. *Compte Rendu* . . . , p. 19.

12. *Al-Istiqlal,* August 4, 1962, p. 3.

13. *Bulletin Officiel du Maroc,* no. 2487, June 24, 1960, "Dahir no. 1-59-315 du 28 hija (23 juin 1959) relatif à l'organisation communale," pp. 1234–35.

14. *Plan Quinquennal,* p. 22.

15. Introductory speech given by Guedira, *La Vigie Marocaine,* June 29, 1961, p. 1.

16. The first director of the National Council for National Promotion was an able official, Messaoudi, now resigned to become governor of Fez early in 1962. He wrote the following report, which criticized the powers and staffing of his group (never more than three well-qualified officials, including one Frenchman). "La Promotion Nationale: Imperatifs et Moyens," December 1961. See also Conseil National de la Promotion Nationale, *But et Bilan,* March 1962, Mimeo.

17. *Journal Officiel de la République Tunisienne,* no. 2, 104e année, "Decret-loi no. 61-4 du 16 janvier 1961 (28 redjeb 1380), insituant un Conseil Economique et Social," p. 69.

18. *Petit Matin,* October 26, 1961, p. 1.

19. Habib Bourguiba, *Bourguiba Addresses the Nation's Leaders,* February 6 and 8, 1961 (Tunis: Secretary of State for Information, 1961).

20. Habib Bourguiba, *Neo-Destourian Socialism,* June 21, 1961 (Tunis: Secretary of State for Information, 1961).

21. *Petit Matin,* November 18, 1961, p. 1.

22. *Ibid.,* November 21, 1961, p. 1.

23. *Ibid.,* December 16, 1961, p. 1.

24. "Le Plan et les Commercants," *Jeune Afrique,* January 23, 1962, pp. 14–15. There may have been an element of passive resistance in a controversy shortly afterward over price controls placed on food imports. See "L'Affaire Tefaha," *ibid.,* March 12–19, 1962, p. 12.

25. *Jeune Afrique,* February 6–12, 1962, p. 6.

26. *Ibid.,* March 26–April 2, 1962, p. 6. Summaries of the speeches are given in this issue. It is unusual for the party to display so forceful a battery of speakers except for congresses and major national holidays.

27. The speeches Bourguiba made on return from a self-imposed retreat following the coup attempt are most revealing. The specific defense appears in "Dimensions of Underdevelopment," Speech of April 14, 1963, to the Sousse Neo-Destour Party School (Tunis: Secretary of State for Cultural Affairs and Information, 1963), p. 15. See also *Accent on Planning,* Speech of March 28, 1963, to the UGTT 9th Congress (Tunis: Secretary of State for Cultural Affairs and Information, 1963).

28. An interesting example is Moroccan and Tunisian plans for chemical plants in conjunction with their phosphate industry. Morocco formulated a plan, announced with great fanfare, several years before Tunisia. Work was held up by poor planning, accusations of corruption, and general discontent over handling the proposal. Last year construction began on a similar Tunisian plant, while Moroccan plans were still confused.

29. See the author's "Tunisian Leadership and the 'Confiscated Revolution,' " *World Politics* (January 1965) for a full exploration of high-level differences over development in the Neo-Destour.

30. Although relatively little field work has been done on attitudinal change in developing countries, the interested reader will find useful suggestions in Milton J. Rosenberg, "A Structural Theory of Attitudinal Change," *Public Opinion Quarterly,* XXIV (Summer 1960), 319–40; R. Abelson, "Modes of Resolution of Belief Dilemmas," *Journal of Conflict Resolution,* III, No. 4 (1959), 343–52.

IV. AN APPROACH THROUGH THE SOCIAL SCIENCES

1. Those interested in pursuing these relationships in political behavior might read A. Campbell, *et al., The American Voter* (New York: Wiley, 1960), pp. 42–119; Gabriel Almond and Sidney Verba, *The Civic Culture* (Princeton: Princeton University Press, 1964); Ulf Himmelstrand, *Social Pressures: Attitudes and the Democratic Process* (Stockholm: Almquist and Wiksell, 1960).

2. See particularly Roger Brown, "Models of Attitude Change," in *New Directions in Social Psychology* (New York: Holt, Rinehart and Winston, 1963), pp. 1–86; Rosenberg, "Structural Theory," pp. 319–40; M. B. Smith, *et al., Opinions and Personality* (New York: Wiley,

1960), pp. 7–28; I. Sarnoff and D. Katz, "The Motivational Basis of Attitude Change," *Journal of Abnormal and Social Psychology, XLIX* (January 1954), 115–24.

3. *The Passing of Traditional Society* (New York: Free Press, 1958), pp. 43–75.

4. The major shortcoming of most of the psychological research in this area is that it is designed for application to postdecisional situations, i.e., a previous behavior is used as the source of attitudinal strain. This has certain advantages in providing the psychologist carefully controlled conditions, but it does not lend itself easily to more general frameworks of perception where specific behaviors are more difficult to single out. See Leon Festinger, *A Theory of Cognitive Dissonance* (Evanston: Row Peterson, 1957); and also John W. Brehm and Arthur R. Cohen, *Explorations in Cognitive Dissonance* (New York: Wiley, 1962).

5. "Communications Patterns and Political Socialization in Transitional Thailand," in Lucian W. Pye, ed., *Communications and Political Development* (Princeton: Princeton Unversity Press, 1963), pp. 184–228.

Selected Bibliography

GOVERNMENT DOCUMENTS

Government of Tunisia, Secretary of State for Planning and Finance. *Perspective Décennale Tunisienne.* 1962.

———. *Plan Triennal (1962–64).* 1962.

———. *Rapport d'Exécution du Plan Triennal.* 1965.

Kingdom of Morocco, Délégation Générale à la Promotion Nationale et au Plan. *Promotion Nationale au Maroc.* 1964.

Kingdom of Morocco, Division of Economic Coordination and Planning. *L'Evolution Economique du Maroc.* 1958.

Kingdom of Morocco, Division of Economic Coordination and Planning. *La Situation Economique du Maroc 1961–62.* 1962.

———. *Plan Biennal d'Equipement 1958–1959.* 1958.

———. *Plan Quinquennal 1960–1964,* n.d. [1960].

Kingdom of Morocco, Division of Economic Coordination and Planning. *Plan Quinquennal: 1960–1964; Le Développement Industriel.* 1962.

Republic of France, General Commissariat of the Plan, Deuxième Plan de Modernisation et d'Equipment. *Rapport Général de la Commission d'Etude et de Coordination des Plans de Modernisation et d'Equipement de l'Algérie, de la Tunisie et du Maroc.* 1954.

BOOKS AND MONOGRAPHS

Ashford, Douglas E. *The Elusiveness of Power: The African Single Party State.* Ithaca: Center of International Studies (Cornell University), 1965.

———. *Perspectives of a Moroccan Nationalist.* Totowa (N.J.): Bedminster Press, 1963.

———. *Political Change in Morocco.* Princeton: Princeton University Press, 1961.

Assouline, Albert. *La Planification Economique et Sociale au Maroc.* Rabat, 1962 (mimeo).

Bourguiba, Habib. *Accent on Planning* (Speech of March 28, 1963 to UGTT Congress). Tunis: Secretary of State for Information, 1963.

———. *Dimensions of Underdevelopment* (Speech of April 14, 1963 to Sousse Neo-Destour Party School). Tunis: Secretary of State for Information, 1963.

Brace, Richard M. *Morocco, Algeria and Tunisia.* Englewood Cliffs: Prentice Hall, 1964.

Cowan, L. Gray. *The Economic Development of Morocco.* Santa Monica: The Rand Corporation, 1958.

Debbasch, Charles. *La République Tunisienne.* Paris: Librairie Générale de Droit et de Jurisprudence, 1962.

Dresch, J., et al. *Industrialisation au Maghreb.* Paris: François Maspéro, 1963.

————. *Reforme Agraire au Maghreb.* Paris: François Maspéro, 1962.

Fadli, Mohammed. *Opération Labour.* Rabat: Centre d'Etude de Développement Economique et Social, 1961.

Gallagher, Charles F. *The United States and North Africa.* Cambridge: Harvard University Press, 1963.

Guen, Moncef. *La Tunisie Indépendante face à son Economie.* Tunis: Cercle d'Etudes Economiques, 1961.

Micaud, Charles A., Carl Brown, and Clement H. Moore. *Tunisia: The Politics of Modernization.* New York: Praeger, 1964.

Moore, Clement H. *Tunisia Since Independence: The Dynamics of One-Party Government.* Berkeley: University of California, 1965.

Robert, Jacques. *La Monarchie Marocaine.* Paris: Librairie Générale de Droit et de Jurisprudence, 1963.

Waterston, Albert. *Planning in Morocco.* Baltimore: Johns Hopkins University Press, 1962.

Zartman, I. William. *Destiny of a Dynasty: The Search for Institutions in Morocco's Developing Society.* Studies in International Affairs, No. 3. Columbia: University of South Carolina, 1964.

————. *Government and Politics in Northern Africa.* New York: Praeger, 1963.

————. *Problems of New Power: Morocco.* New York: Atherton Press, 1964.

ARTICLES

Ashford, Douglas E. "Nation-Building and Nationalism in the Middle East." *Middle East Journal.* Vol. 18, Autumn 1964, pp. 421–30.

————. "National Organizations and Political Development in Morocco," *Il Politico.* Vol. 28, No. 2, June 1963, pp. 360–74.

————. "Tunisian Leadership and the 'Confiscated Revolution'." In *French Speaking Africa,* ed. William H. Lewis. New York: Walker and Co., 1965, pp. 80–91.

Bauchet, P. "Note Rélative aux investissements groupés et diffus au

Maroc." *Cahiers de l'Institut de Science Economique Appliquée.* No. 109 (Series F, No. 16), January 1961, pp. 77–83.

Brunet, Jean. "L'Office National des Irrigations au Maroc, deux ans d'experience." *Annuaire d'Afrique du Nord.* Paris: Centre National de la Recherche Scientifique, 1963, pp. 249–68.

Callens, M. "La Planification Tunisienne." *I.B.L.A.* Vol. 26, No. 101, 1963, pp. 63–73.

Clerc, F. "Rentabilité de l'Opération Labour." *Bulletin Economique et Sociale du Maroc.* No. 82, 1959, pp. 105–72.

Filali, M. "Difficultés et insuffisances de l'économie Tunisienne: essais de solutions." *Cahiers de l'Institut de Science Economique Appliquée.* No. 109 (Series F, No. 16), January 1961, pp. 53–71.

Goussault, Yves. "La Participation des collectivités rurales au développement." *Tiers-Monde.* Tome ii, No. 5, January–March 1961, pp. 236–40.

Marthelot, Pierre. "Histoire et Réalité de la Modernisation du monde rural au Maroc," *Tiers-Monde.* Tome ii, No. 6, April–June 1961, pp. 137–68.

———. "Les implications humaines de l'irrigation moderne en Afrique du Nord." *Annuarie d'Afrique du Nord.* Paris: Centre National de la Recherche Scientifique, 1963, pp. 127–54.

———. "Juxtaposition en Tunisie d'une économie traditionelle et d'une economie moderne," *I.B.L.A.* Vol. 18, No. 4, 1955, pp. 481–501.

M.E.L. "Les institutions du Maroc indépendant et le 'Model Français'." *Tiers-Monde.* Tome ii, No. 6, April–June 1961, pp. 169–82.

Moore, Clement H. "The Neo-Destour: A Structure for Democracy?" *World Politics.* Vol. 14, No. 3, April 1962, pp. 461–82.

Nicolai, André. "Tunisie: fiscalité et développement." *Tiers-Monde.* Vol. 3, No. 11, July–September 1962, pp. 429–78.

Oved, Georges. "Problèmes du développement économique au Maroc." *Tiers-Monde.* Tome ii, No. 7, July–November 1961, pp. 355–98.

Tiano, André. "Une expérience de mobilisation du travail au Maroc." *Cahiers de l'Institut de Science Economique Appliquée.* No. 122 (Series AB, No. 2), February 1962.

———. "La Politique economique et financière du Maroc Indépendant." *Tiers-Monde* (Etudes), 1963.

Zanouni, M. "Le rôle de l'administration dans l'exécution du Plan." *Aspects et Perspectives de l'Economie Tunisienne.* Vol. 2, No. 2, March–April 1962, pp. 37–71.

Zarka, Claude. "L'économie Tunisienne á l'heure de la planification impérative." *Annuaire d'Afrique du Nord.* Centre National de la Recherche Scientifique, 1963, pp. 207–42.

Index

Alaouite Dynasty: 45; Istiqlal loyalty to, 32

Algerian Revolution, Tunisian involvement, 18, 22, 25

Allal Al-Fassi, 9, 32

American surplus wheat: in Tunisian public works projects, 24–25; in Moroccan public relief program, 36

Bahi, Ladgham, 41

Balafrej, 15, 52n

Banque Centrale, 21

Banque du Commerce Extérieur, 15

Banque du Maroc, 15

Ben Barka, 14

Ben Salah, Ahmed: Secretary General of *L'Union Générale des Travailleurs Tunisiennes*, 21; Minister of Public Health and Labor, 22, 23, 24; head of planning organization, 27, 28, 38, 39, 40

Ben Seddiq, Mahjoub, 14

Ben Youssef, Salah, 20, 21

Bey of Tunis, removal by Bourguiba, 20, 21, 22

Bizerte, Tunisia, 40

Bouabid, Abderahim: 14, 15, 16, 28, 31, 36, 54n; head of ministries for economic problems, 12; letter to king requesting delegation of powers, 15, 52n; Istiqlal leader, 33

Bourguiba, Habib: reconciliation with Ben Salah, 23; Neo-Destour organization, 24, 53n; assassination attempt in 1962, 42, 55–56n; mentioned *passim*

Bourguibism, 39

Businessmen. *See* Merchants of Tunisia

Casablanca, Morocco, 20, 33, 34, 54n

Central Bank, of Tunisia, 43

Commissariat du Plan, 4

Commissariat Général du Plan, 10

Communism: 1, 33; Bourguiba's attitude to, 39, 55n

Demographic growth, 32

Destourian socialism, 2

Douiri, Mohammed: Minister of Public Works and Housing, 12; Minister of National Economy, 16, 32, 33, 34, 36, 54n, 55n

France: administrative practice in North Africa, 4; Metropole, 4; Protectorate, 9, 12, 18, 19; planning in Tunisia, 10, 19; ten-year plan, 1947–56, 10. *See also Commissariat du Plan*

Ghafsa, Tunisia, 19

Gharb plain, Morocco, 12

"Gradualism," Bourguiba's policy of, 40

Habous, 21, 39, 55n

Hached, Farhat, 20

Hassan, King Moulay II: 16, 31; political methods, 32, 34, 37, 45, 54–55n

Ibrahim, Abdullah, 15, 16, 33

Imam, 45

Istiqlal: 5–19, 33–36 *passim*; Sfax Congress of 1955, 20; Congress of 1960, 32, 54n

Laghzaoui, 34

Lerner, Daniel, 47, 56n

L'Union Générale des Travailleurs Tunisiennes (UGTT): 21, 22, 25, 26, 27, 38; Congress report of 1956, 21, 22, 23, 27, 42, 52n;

L'Union Générale (*continued*)
    Eighth National Congress of 1960,
    25, 26; *On the Difficult Road to
    Development*, 26, 54n
L'Union Marocaine d'Agriculture,
    13
*L'Union Marocaine de l'Industrie,
    de Commerce et d'Artisanat*, 13,
L'Union Marocaine du Travail
    (UMT), 13, 14, 20, 31, 33
*L'Union Tunisienne de l'Industrie et
    du Commerce*, 26–27
Lyautey, Marshal, 9

Maghrib, 11, 19
Marshall Plan, 10, 19
Mejerda Valley project, 19
Merchants of Tunisia, reaction to
    plan, 27, 40, 41, 42, 55n
Mesadi, 25
Metropole. *See* France
Mohammed V: 9, 16, 22; meeting
    with Roosevelt, 10; death of, 31
Monarchy, influence in planning, 8
Morocco: Ministry of Finance, 4;
    political indecision, 8; Marshall
    Plan, 10; Office for Research and
    Participation in Mining, 10; Plan-
    ning Office, 11; Superior Planning
    Council, 13, 14, 16, 23, 35, 52n;
    Division for Economic Coordina-
    tion and the Plan, 13, 14, 16, 28,
    52n; Office for Industrial Research
    and Participation, 15; five-year
    plan of 1960, 16, 17, 34–35, 52n;
    planning activity, 17, 32–37, 41,
    44, 45, 54n; Directorate of Eco-
    nomic Coordination and Planning,
    31; elections, 31; Ministry of the
    National Economy, 31–32, -and
    Finance, 35; three-year proposal,
    34, 54n; National Office of Irriga-
    tion, 35; National Office of Rural
    Modernization, 35; *Promotion
    Nationale*, 36, 37, 55n
Mosel, James N., 48

National Bank for Economic Devel-
    opment (*Banque Nationale pour
    le Développement Economique*),
    15

National Front, of Tunisia, 38, 55n
National planning: 2, 5, 6, 51n;
    political doctrine, 3, 7; attitudinal
    change, 46, 47, 48, 51n, 56n; so-
    cial science approach, 46–49, 56–
    57n; institutionalized change, 48
National Union (*L'Union National
    des Forces Populaires*), 16, 17, 28,
    31, 33
Nationalism, 1, 3, 4, 5, 51n
Neo-Destour: 4, 38, 43; 18–27
    passim; renamed Constitutionalist
    Socialist Party, 8; Political Bu-
    reau, 20, 39, 52n; Sfax Congress
    of, 20, 52n; Sousse Congress of,
    25, 53n; as "socialist" party, 26,
    39, 41, 54n; National Council, 40,
    41, 55n
Nouira, Hedi, 21, 43

Office of European Economic Coop-
    eration (OEEC), 4
"Operation Plow," 15, 52n

Protectorate. *See* France

Rabat, Tunisia, 35
Regional planning, 35, 36, 55n
Roosevelt, Franklin D., 10
Rural communes, 36, 55n

Sahel, Tunisia, 19
Sakiet-Sidi-Youssef attack, 22
Sfax, Tunisia, 19, 52n
Sherifian Phosphate Office, 9
Single-party system, 8, 18, 22, 23,
    35, 38–44
Sousse, Tunisia, 19, 52n
Syndicats, 36

Thailand, 48
Tilili, 22, 52n
Tunis, 18, 38, 43
Tunisia: four-year plans, 19; Grand
    Council of Tunisia, 19, 52n; labor
    movement, 19–20; Constituent As-
    sembly, 21; National Planning
    Council, 22, 23, 24, 26; National
    Assembly, 23, 25, 40, 41; Ministry
    of Education's ten-year plan, 25,
    43, 53n; Directorate of Planning,

26; Federation of Industry and Commerce report of 1960, 26–27; ten-year plan (*Perspective Décennal*), 26, 31, 38, 42, 43; Ministry of Industry and Commerce, 28; planning activity, 30, 31, 41, 44, 48, 49, 56n; Ministry of Interior, 36, 43; Economic and Social Council, 38, 40, 55n; three-year plan (*Plan Triennal*), 38, 41; Planning Commission, 38, 40, 55n; Secretariat for Planning and Finance, 38; Political Bureau, 40; Ministry of Public Works, 43

UMT. *See L'Union Marocaine du Travail*
United Nations, 28
United States, 10
Unions, American, 21